Using
PowerPoint
IN THE
Classroom

Using
PowerPoint
IN THE
Classroom

Dusti Howell
Deanne Howell

With contributions from:
Jean Morrow
Armand Seguin
Jennifer Summerville

CORWIN PRESS, INC.
A Sage Publications Company
Thousand Oaks, California

For information:

Corwin Press, Inc.
A Sage Publications Company
2455 Teller Road
Thousand Oaks, California 91320
E-mail: order@corwinpress.com

Sage Publications Ltd.
6 Bonhill Street
London EC2A 4PU
United Kingdom

Sage Publications India Pvt. Ltd.
M-32 Market
Greater Kailash I
New Delhi 110 048 India

Printed in the United States of America

Library of Congress Cataloging-in-Publication Data

Using PowerPoint in the classroom / by Dusti Howell ... [et al.].
    p. cm.
    Includes index.
    ISBN 0-7619-7881-X — ISBN 0-7619-7882-8 (pbk.)
    1. Microsoft PowerPoint (Computer file) 2. Computer managed instruction. 3. Computer-assisted instruction.   I. Howell, Dusti.
    LB1028.46 .U83 2002
    006.6'869—dc21

                                    2001005565

This book is printed on acid-free paper.

    03   04   05   06   07   7   6   5   4   3

Acquisitions Editor:	Robb Clouse
Associate Editor:	Kylee Liegl
Editorial Assistant:	Erin Buchanan
Production Editor:	Olivia Weber
Typesetter/Designer:	Larry K. Bramble
Copy Editor:	Denise McIntyre
Cover Designer:	Tracy E. Miller

Contents

Preface

Welcome to *Using PowerPoint in the Classroom.* If you want to create more dynamic classroom lessons and presentations using quick and easy custom animations, this book is for you. The focus of this book is to explain the use of transitions, graphics, charts, graphs, and sound effects in a format that makes learning fun. This book is designed to give you immediate results using either Windows or Macintosh platforms. You will also learn the fundamentals of designing effective slides while discovering great ways to use PowerPoint in your own classroom.

Acknowledgments

We would like to extend our sincere appreciation to our colleagues in the field and in the classroom who read this text, tested our ideas, and provided feedback and support during the editorial process.

The following reviewers are gratefully acknowledged:

Gregg Elder
Teacher-Librarian, Technical Chair
Evergreen Middle School
Everett, WA

Joe Meersman
Teacher
Toppenish High School
Toppenish, WA

Robin Van Heyningen
Teacher
White River High School
Buckley, WA

Richard J. Marchesani
Assistant Professor of Education
Elmira College
Elmira, NY

Kristen L. Blake
Teacher
La Habra High School
La Habra, CA

Eric Alm
Teacher
Jenkins High School
Chewelah, WA

Katherine Avila
Teacher
Tewksbury Memorial High School
Tewksbury, MA

Ken Martin
Coordinator of Curriculum and
    Instruction
University of Cincinnati
College of Education
Cincinnati, OH

Blake West
District Coordinating Teacher for
    Technology
Blue Valley Schools
Overland Park, KS

Ellen Thompson
Teacher
Horizon Elementary School
Madison, AL

Fred MacDonald
Program Officer
Standards of Practice and
    Education
Ontario College of Teachers
Toronto, Ontario
Canada

Tawn Rundle
Teacher/Elementary Technology
    Coordinator
Laverne Public Schools

Note: All screen shots are reprinted
by permission of Microsoft Corporation

About the Authors

Dusti D. Howell earned a PhD in curriculum and instruction with an emphasis in educational communications and technology and a PhD minor in educational psychology from the University of Wisconsin–Madison. He is currently teaching at Emporia State University in the Instructional Design and Technology Department. His expertise includes high-tech study skills and digital learning strategies, multimedia, and video production. He teaches online courses including "Powerful Presentations in PowerPoint" and "Fundamental 4Mat Training." He has taught every grade level from first grade through graduate school. He is currently President of the local chapter of Phi Delta Kappa.

Deanne K. Howell teaches professional development courses for university faculty and staff. She conducts professional development workshops, online courses, and classes for Emporia State University. Deanne holds a master's degree in science education from the University of Wisconsin–Madison. She has taught in public, private, and international schools.

Jean Morrow, OSM, EdD, has 40 years of classroom teaching experience at all levels, from first grade through university. Jean has been a member of Servants of Mary since 1958. She earned a master's degree in mathematics education from the University of Detroit and a PhD in instructional design and technology from Boston University. The coauthor of two books on mathematics instruction, she is a frequent speaker at state and national meetings. Her favorite theme for those talks is the integration of technology and problem solving. Most recently, Jean has been teaching classes over the Internet for Emporia State University. Jean serves on the Board of Examiners for the National Council for the Accreditation of Teacher Education. In 1998, she was given the Distinguished Clinician Award in Teacher Education by the Association of Teacher Educators.

Armand Seguin is Associate Professor and Chair of the Department of Instructional Design and Technology at Emporia State University. He is keenly interested in the impact of technology on the classroom teacher and was an early adopter of the Apple IIe. Other interests include teaching via distance learning. He initiated one of the first online courses in the country when he delivered Electronic Mail for Educators via the Alaska Computer Network in 1986. He has delivered many professional presentations and is active in the Association for Teacher Educators and chaired its Commission on Utilizing Technology in Educational Reform. He holds membership in the Association for Educational Communications & Technology, the Society for Information Technology in Education, and the Mid-America Association for Computers in Education. He holds an EdD from Arizona State University, a master's degree from Indiana State University, and a bachelor's from St. Cloud State University. He has taught at Dakota State University, University of Alaska Southeast, Jackson State University, and West Virginia State College.

Jennifer Summerville is Assistant Professor of Instructional Design and Technology at Emporia State University. Jennifer specializes in instructional design, distance education, and instructional media design. She received a master's degree in computer education and cognitive systems from the University of North Texas and a PhD in educational technology with emphasis in distance education, instructional design, and interactive multimedia design from the University of Northern Colorado. Her research interests include integration of technology in the K-12 classroom, learner-centered issues in distance education, and cognitive and personality issues in the design and development of instruction.

From Dusti and Deanne Howell

To our children Autumn and Trevor
who never cease to amaze us,
and to our little son Kit,
who was born shortly after
we wrote this book.

**CORWIN
PRESS**

The Corwin Press logo—a raven striding across an open book—represents the happy union of courage and learning. We are a professional-level publisher of books and journals for K-12 educators, and we are committed to creating and providing resources that embody these qualities. Corwin's motto is "Success for All Learners."

Introduction to Microsoft® PowerPoint®

*T*his book covers Microsoft Windows versions 97 and 2000 and Macintosh versions 98 and 2000 of PowerPoint. These versions are very similar with minor differences, containing most of the same commands, toolbars, and menus. Once you become familiar with using one version, adapting to another version is relatively easy.

One important difference between the Macintosh and Windows version is the keyboard shortcuts. Windows uses the **Ctrl** key, the equivalent of the **Command ⌘** key on the Macintosh. While holding down **Ctrl** or **Command ⌘** press a particular key (e.g., "S" for "Save") to execute a task. The directions for this shortcut look like this: **Ctrl/⌘ + S**.

Most of the directions in this book work for all four versions. When there are differences, look for the following:

WIN or WINDOWS   Windows versions 97 and 2000 only

MAC or MACINTOSH   Macintosh versions 98 and 2000 only

WIN 97   Windows version 97 only

WIN 00   Windows 2000 only

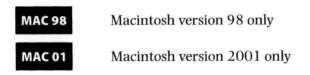

MAC 98   Macintosh version 98 only

MAC 01   Macintosh version 2001 only

Please note: By using the step-by-step directions in the chapters, you will create a comprehensive slide show complete with custom animations, sounds, and transitions. The instructions in each chapter build on the previous chapters. Should you wish to skip or omit a section, you will need to create the slides as shown in the illustrations.

This Book Contains the Following Helpful Features

✔ **Troubleshooting Tips:** Includes possible problems you may encounter and alternative methods for performing the task. Time-saving tips will also be found here.

☞ **Learn More:** Experiment and try out the suggested ideas to become more proficient with PowerPoint.

What PowerPoint Version Am I Using?

To find out exactly which version you are using on the Windows platform, you will need to launch PowerPoint (see the section Launching PowerPoint).

WIN

Click on **Help** and then select **About Microsoft PowerPoint** from the drop-down menu.

MAC

Click on the **Apple Menu** (top left of screen) and select **About Microsoft PowerPoint**.

An information box will appear indicating the particular version installed on your computer.

Using the Mouse

The standard mouse is different for Windows and Macintosh users. PowerPoint for Windows makes use of two buttons on the mouse, the left and right, with the left button being the primary control, whereas the mouse for Macintosh users has only one button. Before jumping into *Using PowerPoint*, you should be familiar with just a few terms.

MOUSE CLICK

WIN

Press the *left* mouse button.

MAC

Simply click on the mouse button.

RIGHT CLICK

WIN

Press down the *right* button on the mouse.

MAC

While holding down the **Ctrl** key on the keyboard press the mouse button: **Ctrl + Click**.

DOUBLE CLICK

WIN

Rapidly press the left mouse button twice.

MAC

Rapidly press the mouse button twice.

DRAG AND DROP

Press and hold down the mouse button while simultaneously moving the mouse. Release the mouse after highlighting the desired text, selecting a menu item option, or moving an object to a desired location.

Launching PowerPoint

PowerPoint is opened the same way other Microsoft applications are opened. The biggest difference between the Windows and Macintosh platforms is the way the application is initially launched.

WINDOWS

1. The most common way to launch is to put the cursor on the **Start** button on the far left of the task bar at the bottom of the screen.

2. Click on the mouse and the Start window will pop up. Continue holding the button down while scrolling up to the **Programs** folder.

3. Scroll through the list of programs and click on **Microsoft PowerPoint** to automatically launch the program.

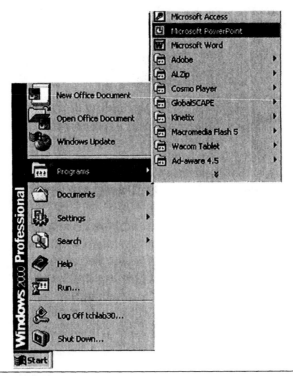

Figure 1.1   Windows Start Up

PowerPoint will appear on the screen. In the top right corner of the screen, notice two rows of the following three buttons.

The top row of buttons affects the PowerPoint program whereas the bottom row only affects the current PowerPoint slide show. In the top row, the **Minimize** button to the left will collapse the window to a button on the Windows task bar. The **Restore/Maximize** button increases or decreases the size of the presentation window. The **Close** button exits PowerPoint. The **Close** button in the second row only closes the current slide show, but leaves PowerPoint open.

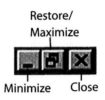

Restore/
Maximize

Minimize   Close

MACINTOSH

Double click the Hard Drive—often labeled **Macintosh HD**—icon at the top right of the screen to bring up the Macintosh Hard Drive window that indicates all of the programs and documents stored on your computer's hard drive.

1. Double click on the **Microsoft Office** folder. The Microsoft Office window will appear.

2. Double click on the icon labeled **Microsoft PowerPoint**.

If you have used PowerPoint recently, click on the **Apple** menu located at the top left of the screen to bring down the menu. Go down to **Recent Applications** and click **Microsoft PowerPoint** to open up the application.

The top row of the work area window is called the **Title Bar**. The **Close Box** on the far left of this bar closes the window when clicked. Note: It does not close PowerPoint—it is still open when the Application menu in the top right corner of the screen is selected. Two other buttons are located on the far right side of the title bar. The first is the **Zoom Box** that changes the size of the window when clicked. The **Collapse Box** in the far right corner collapses the window but leaves the title bar open on the screen.

Zoom

Close   Collapse

Four Options for Working in PowerPoint

When PowerPoint is first opened, the dialog box in Figure 1.2 will appear with four options for beginning PowerPoint. Choose an option by selecting one of the buttons on the left, then click **OK**.

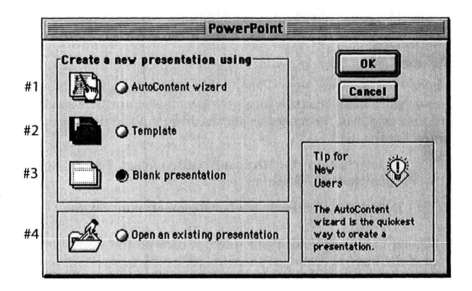

Figure 1.2   Initial Dialog Box

MAC 01

MAC 2001 version opens with the Project Gallery dialog box. The same four options can be accessed from the Gallery.

✔**Troubleshooting Tip:** If the Project Gallery dialog box fails to come up, select **File > Project Gallery**.

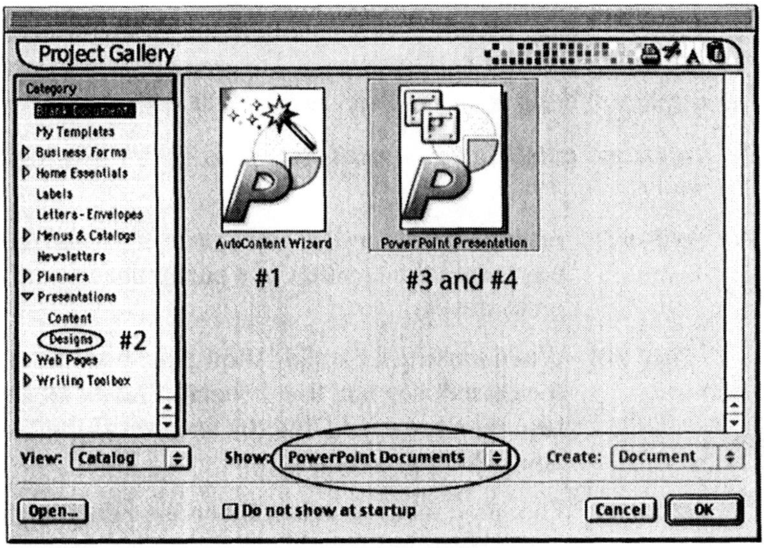

Figure 1.3 Mac 2001 Project Gallery Dialog Box

ALL VERSIONS

1. The **AutoContent Wizard** is a quick and easy method for creating a slide show. It provides a series of questions to create an instant slide show to be edited. The AutoContent Wizard is ideal when brainstorming or outlining a presentation, however, most of the templates are geared toward business. The Wizard gives step-by-step directions.

   MAC 01: To find this option, click on the *show* drop-down box at the bottom of the Project Gallery dialog box and choose *PowerPoint Documents*. Make sure *Blank Documents* is chosen in the *Category* window on the left.

2. Choose **Design Templates** or **Template** to build a slide show using a predesigned slide containing a color scheme, type style, matching bullets, and other elements.

   MAC 01: The **Designs Template** is located in the *Category* window under *Presentations*. Click on the small rectangle to the left of *Presentations* to view the subcategories, and then click on *Designs*.

3. **Blank presentation** creates a blank (white) slide for a presentation. Generally, this option is used to create a slide show from scratch. A design template can be added at any time.

4. **Open an existing presentation** opens up an existing slide show.

   WIN 97: Browse to open a slide show using the *Open* dialog box to find the location of a particular PowerPoint presentation.

   MAC 98: When looking for a slide show that is not listed in the *Open* dialog box that appears, choose **Desktop**, then browse to find the location of the PowerPoint presentation.

   WIN 00: The small window below **Open an existing presentation** contains the most recent slide shows that have been opened. Double clicking on any of them opens the file. To open other presentations, select *More Files* at the top of the list, then **OK** and navigate to the file's location in the *Open* dialog box.

   MAC 01: Double click on *PowerPoint Presentation.* Click on **Cancel** when the New Slide dialog box appears. To open up an existing presentation, select **File > Open**.

Understanding Menus, Icons (Buttons), and Keyboard Commands

WIN & MAC

There is generally more than one way to perform a task in PowerPoint, allowing the user to work in the manner preferred.

Menus, icons, or a keyboard shortcut can often be used to perform the same task. Menus are located on the top bar and almost always start with the options File, Edit,and View. Click on a menu item to view the drop-down menu selection. Icons are graphically illustrated "buttons" located on the bars below the Menu and perform specific tasks. For example, save work by selecting **File >** **Save** from the menu, or press the **Save**

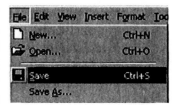

 icon, or choose **Ctrl/⌘ + S** from the keyboard. Hold down the **Ctrl (MAC: ⌘)** key while pressing **S** on the keyboard.

WIN 00 & MAC 01

In version 2000 and 2001, the drop-down menu may be "folded." To view the full drop-down menu, click on the double arrows or hold your cursor above the arrows until the menu expands.

More Buttons on Menu

Full Drop-Down Menu

These versions also contain more icons on the toolbar, many which remain hidden behind the **More** or "expand" buttons. Notice the More buttons on the 2000 Standard and Formatting toolbars. The most frequently used tools remain visible at the top of the screen whereas less used buttons move behind the "expand" buttons to reduce screen cluster. When a particular icon cannot be found, be sure to click on the More buttons.

More Buttons

Toolbars

Before beginning, make sure you have the needed toolbars on your screen. Each toolbar contains a series of buttons that perform specific tasks. Select **View** and choose **Toolbars** from the drop-down menu. Select **Standard**, **Formatting**, and **Drawing** (each one should have a check in front of it). These are the toolbars you will use most often in this program.

 Learn More: Context-based toolbars often appear on the screen automatically when you are working with particular features in

PowerPoint. For example, when adding ClipArt from the MS Gallery, the Picture toolbar may appear on the screen, allowing you to easily modify the graphics. Likewise, when working with WordArt on a slide, the WordArt toolbar may open. At other times, the desired toolbars will need to be opened manually.

Below the Menu toolbar is the Standard toolbar that contains graphically illustrated buttons for common tasks such as starting a new slide show, opening up a preexisting slide show, and printing, saving, and spell checking. The Formatting toolbar contains buttons used for formatting text such as changing the type of font (style of print) and size, bolding, italicizing, underlining, and aligning text.

Undoing Mistakes

How do I get back if I make a mistake? Undo and Redo are generally the first two options in the Edit menu. Notice the keyboard shortcuts for these commands.

Click on the **Undo** icon or **Ctrl/⌘ + Z** to undo any prior mistakes, or redo the action by clicking on the **Redo** icon or **Ctrl/⌘ + Y**. The down arrow next to the Undo and Redo icons allows you to quickly "go back" to the exact action you wish to change.

Edit Menu selections   Keyboard shortcuts   Undo and Redo icons

✔ **Troubleshooting Tip:** The Undo and Redo commands are very limited with charts, graphs, and tables. You may only have one level of undo.

What Does This Button Do?

Want to know the label for each button? Hold the cursor over each button briefly until its name appears in a yellow text box just below each button.

Want to learn more about the function of each button?

WINDOWS

Select **Help** and select **What's This**? A question mark will appear next to the cursor. Press on any icon to see a brief description of its function.

MACINTOSH

Select **Help** and select **Balloon Help**. A description of the function for each icon will appear in a callout or balloon as your cursor moves over each icon.

Help Is Only a Click Away

The Office Assistant is an animated character that can answer your questions and provide tips and suggestions as you work. The default character is either an animated paper clip or a computer.

If the Office Assistant is not visible when opening up PowerPoint, click on the **Help** icon on the Standard toolbar. The Office Assistant can be turned off at any time by *right* clicking **(MAC: Ctrl + Click)** on the Assistant and choosing **Hide** or **Hide Assistant** from the drop-down menu. The Office Assistant can be moved out of your way by dragging and dropping it to a new location on the screen.

 **Learn More:** As you work, the Office Assistant may provide helpful tips. A yellow light bulb will appear near the Office Assistant indicating that it has a suggestion. Click on the yellow light bulb to view the tip.

Use the Office Assistant to look up or find answers to topics or questions.

1. Click on the Office Assistant to bring up the callout window.

2. Type a question, phrase, or word in the callout window. For example, look up

keyboard shortcuts. Type "keyboard shortcuts" in the window and then select **Search**. A list of related topics will appear below. Select *Use Keyboard Shortcuts* to bring up the index of keyboard shortcuts.

3. Click on any of the entries to learn more.

Quick Review

► **What PowerPoint Version Am I Using?**

WIN: Help > About Microsoft PowerPoint

MAC: Apple > About Microsoft PowerPoint

► **Using the Mouse:**

Right clicking in Windows is the same as holding down Ctrl and clicking in MAC.

Drag and Drop Hold down the mouse button while simultaneously moving the mouse

► **Launching PowerPoint:**

WIN: Start > Programs > PowerPoint

MAC: Double click on Hard drive icon > double click on MS Office folder > double click on PowerPoint

► **Four Options for Working in PowerPoint:**

AutoContent Wizard, Template, Blank Presentation, Open an Existing Presentation

► **Standard Toolbars Used:**

View > Toolbars, select Standard, Formatting, and Drawing

► **Common Tools:**

Undo: Edit > Undo, Undo icon, or Ctrl/⌘ + Z
Redo: Edit > Redo, Redo icon, or Ctrl/⌘ + Y

▶ **What Does This Button Do?**

WIN: Help > What's This?

MAC: Help > Show Balloons

▶ **Help Options/Office Assistant:**

Turn on *Office Assistant* with
the *Help* icon

Click on *Office Assistant* then
type in topic or question,
Enter/Return then click on topic to learn more

▶ **Turn Off Assistant:**

WIN   *Right* click > Hide

MAC   Ctrl + Click > Hide

▶ **Other Information:**

The **(WIN)** Ctrl key is the same as the **(MAC)** Command ⌘ key

2

Creating a New Slide Show

Book Report Scenario

Teachers often assign students a book report project. With PowerPoint, teachers can have each student deliver a multimedia presentation on the book report instead of the traditional written report. Step-by-step directions will be given on creating a sample book report presentation of *The Lorax* by Dr. Seuss (1971, Random House: New York).

Creating the Title Slide

Choosing a Slide Layout

After initially opening PowerPoint:

1. Select **Blank Presentation**, then **OK.**

    MAC 01: Double click on **Blank Presentation**. (See Figure 1.2.) The **New Slide** dialog box will appear.

2. The slide show will begin with a title slide. Double click on the first *Slide Layout* (AutoLayout), the *Title Slide*, to select it, or click once on the *Title Slide* and press **OK.** This title slide contains two placeholders, one for the title and another for the subtitle.

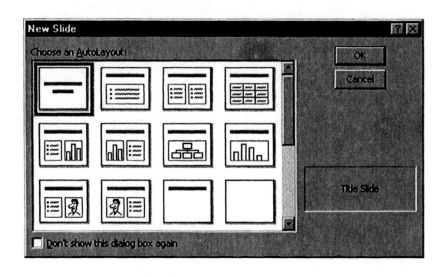

Figure 2.1 Slide Layout Dialog Box

> **WIN 00:** Find the **Slide Layout** icon under **Common Tasks** on the **Formatting** toolbar.

 Learn More: Each *Slide Layout* will automatically place and size the title, text, clip art, graphs, objects, and movies within placeholders on the slide. There are 24 slide layouts. Use the vertical scroll bar to the right to view more options.

✔**Troubleshooting Tip:** If the **Slide Layout** dialog box does not appear, click on the **Slide Layout** icon.

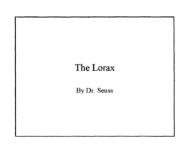

Versions 97, 98, & 2000

Version 2001

3. Click on the box that says *Click to add title* and type "The Lorax." For the subtitle type "By Dr. Seuss."

The Lorax

By Dr. Seuss

Spell Checking

Notice the red squiggly line under the word "Lorax." Microsoft has an automatic spell checker that alerts you to possible misspellings. *Right* click (**MAC: Ctrl + Click**) on the word "Lorax" to view suggested replacements for the word. Because "Lorax" is a proper name, the spell checker's dictionary simply does not recognize the word. When you want to replace your word with one of the suggested words, click on one of the suggested words.

Learn More: The spell checker's dictionary is limited. Words underlined in red are not necessarily misspelled. If in doubt, consult a regular dictionary.

Understanding Slide Panes and Slide Views

WIN 97 & MAC 98

Versions 97 or 98 open in **Slide View** as one large slide with no panes.

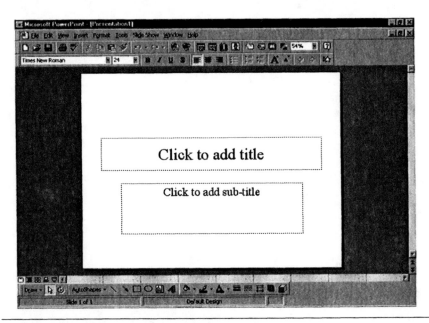

Figure 2.2   Full Screen Slide View 97

WIN 00 & MAC 01

Versions 2000 and 2001 are divided into three sections called panes:
Slide Pane, Outline Pane, and Notes Pane.

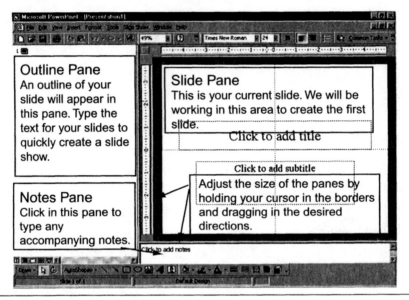

Figure 2.3 Full Screen Normal View 2000

Slide Views

ALL VERSIONS

At the bottom left of the screen, notice the five small icons.

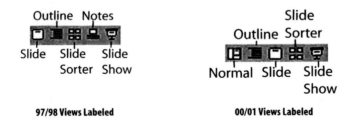

97/98 Views Labeled   **00/01 Views Labeled**

Normal View (**WIN 00 & MAC 01 only**) divides the screen
into three nearly equal sections. Work directly on a slide in the
slide pane, add text quickly to a show using the *Outline* pane,

and add speaker's notes in the *Notes* pane. For many, this is the most useful view because it contains all of the features available in *Slide, Outline,* and *Notes* view.

Outline View is best for adding text to slides. This view is ideal for adding, deleting, and moving slides. Look at the titles in a glance and create an instant summary slide. This view is especially useful for converting one's notes into an instant slide show.

Slide View is used for adding all elements (text, graphics, animations, movies, graphs, charts, and other objects) to a slide.

Slide Sorter View is for viewing all slides with text and graphics on one screen. This view is useful for adding, deleting, and moving slides. In addition, animation and transition effects can be added in this view.

Slide Show View is used for presenting slides on a full screen, just as the audience would view them. Listen to all added sounds and view any animations, movies, and transitions on the slides. This view hides the menu and toolbars. To exit this view, press **Esc** on the keyboard.

Notes Page View (**WIN 97** & **MAC 98 only**) is for adding speaker's notes. (Although there is no **Notes Page View** in versions 2000 and 2001, you can add notes in the *Notes* pane that can be found in *Normal, Outline,* and *Slide* views.)

☞ **Learn More:** Take a moment to get comfortable moving between the five views.

Creating the Second and Third Slides

Working in Outline View

The first slide was created in **Slide Show View** (**WIN 97** & **MAC 98**) or **Normal View** (**WIN 00** & **MAC 01**). The next two slides will be created in **Outline View,** the most efficient view for adding text.

1. Select the **Outline View** icon. Note that the title slide you have created is now in outline form. In this view, each slide is numbered with a slide icon to the left. To the right of the **Slide** icon is the title (in larger type) and below the slide icon are the main points.

Slide icon

Slide number �1 **The Lorax** ◄── Slide title

By Dr. Seuss ◄ Main point

2. To effectively work in this view, bring up the **Outlining** toolbar. It will appear on the left vertical border of the screen in versions 97, 98, and 2000 and on a horizontal toolbar in 2001.

✔ **Troubleshooting Tip:** If the Outlining toolbar does not appear, select **View > Toolbars > Outlining**.

At the beginning of the Outlining toolbar are *left* and *right* facing arrows.

Promote one level. This icon moves (promotes) a subpoint up one level to a main point, or moves a main point up one level to become the title. **Shift + Tab** (hold down both the **Shift** and **Tab** keys) also performs the same function.

Promote Icon   01 Promote Icon

Demote one level. This moves (demotes) a title down one level to a main point, a main point down to a subpoint, and so forth. **Tab** does the same function.

Demote Icon   01 Demote Icon

3. Place the cursor just behind the word "Seuss" and press **Enter/Return**.

4. To create a new slide, click on the **Promote** icon **(Shift + Tab)**. Notice a slide icon appears after the number 2 indicating that a new slide was created.

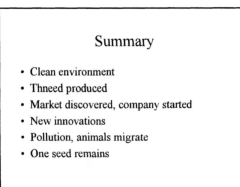

1 ☐ The Lorax
   By Dr. Seuss
2 ☐ Summary
   • Clean environment
   • Thneed produced
   • Market discovered, company started
   • New innovations
   • Pollution, animals migrate
   • One seed remains
3 ☐ Climax
   • All Truffula trees destroyed
   • Polluted environment
      • Truffula fruit shortage
      • Smogulous smoke
      • Smeary water|

5. Type "Summary" then **Enter/Return**.

6. To change Slide 3 from a new slide/title to a main point, click on the **Demote** icon (or **Tab**). After the first bullet, type "Clean Environment" and press **Enter/Return**.

7. After the second bullet, type "Thneed produced," then **Enter/Return**.

Summary

• Clean environment
• Thneed produced
• Market discovered, company started
• New innovations
• Pollution, animals migrate
• One seed remains

---

8. The next four main points (bulleted text) are "Market Discovered, company started," "New innovations," "Pollution, animals migrate," and "One seed remains."

9. After finishing the text for slide 2, press **Enter/Return** again. Another bullet will appear.

10. **Creating Slide 3.** We want to move this main point up one level (promote) to a title on a new slide. Click on the **Promote** icon to bring up the *Slide 3 icon* and type "Climax" then **Enter/Return**.

11. Press the **Demote** icon to create a main point. Type "All Truffula trees destroyed" and press **Enter/Return**.

12. For the second bullet, type "Polluted environment" and press **Enter/Return**.

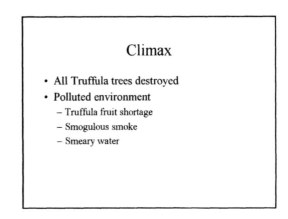

Climax

- All Truffula trees destroyed
- Polluted environment
  - Truffula fruit shortage
  - Smogulous smoke
  - Smeary water

13. Move the third main point down (demote) to a subpoint. Click on the **Demote** icon or **Tab** and type "Truffula fruit shortage," then press **Enter/Return**, type "Smogulous smoke," then press **Enter/Return**, and type "Smeary water," then press **Enter/Return**. Note the bullets have changed and the text has moved to the right indicating a change to subpoints.

Creating the Fourth Slide

Creating Slides in Normal or Slide View

The remaining slides are better developed in **Normal** or **Slide View** because they contain more graphical elements and information presented in more than one column. Click on the **Normal** or **Slide View** icon.

Normal View

Slide View

Troubleshooting Tip: Because Windows 2000 and Macintosh 2001 versions of PowerPoint automatically resize text as more lines are added, it is best to add the text directly into the two-column layout in Slide View, otherwise, you may end up with one long column of text with no text in the second column.

The fourth slide will illustrate how the message of *The Lorax* applies to current environmental problems. This slide contains several main points with subpoints that will not fit nicely in one column.

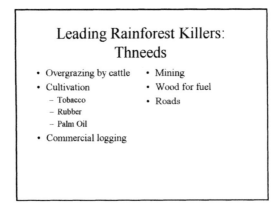

1. Navigate to slide 3. Then add a new slide by clicking on the **New Slide** icon. Note, in the Windows 2000 version three of the most commonly used tools are hidden behind **Common Tasks.**

   WIN 00: **Common Tasks > New Slide.**

2. Select the *2 Column Text* option (third selection in the first row) in the *Slide Layout* dialog box and click **OK.**

3. Type "Leading Rainforest Killers: Thneeds" in the title area.

4. Click in the first column and type "Overgrazing by cattle," then press **Enter/Return.**

5. Type "Cultivation" for the second point, then press **Enter/ Return**.

6. Press **Tab** to indent to a subpoint and type "Tobacco," then press **Enter/Return**, type "Rubber," then press **Enter/ Return**, and type "Palm Oil," then press **Enter/Return**.

7. To return to a main point press **Shift + Tab** and type "Commercial logging."

8. In the second column, we will add three additional main points. Click in the second column and type "Mining," then press **Enter/Return**, type "Wood for fuel," then press **Enter/ Return**, and type "Roads."

✔**Troubleshooting Tip**: In the newest PowerPoint versions for both Windows and Macintosh, adding additional lines of text near the bottom of the slide automatically reduces the font size of all the text to fit the slide. Beware, this reduction of the font size may make it difficult for the audience to read the text when presented.

Saving a Slide Show

Now it is time to save our work.

1. Go to **File > Save As**.

Figure 2.4   2000 Save Dialog Box

Save: Microsoft PowerPoint

Desktop	⬥

	Date Modified	▲
📂 1	4/30/72	
📂 2001	5/5/72	
📂 98	5/5/72	
📄 *Acrobat™ Reader 4.0*	3/31/21	▲
🌐 *Browse the Internet*	3/31/21	▼

Name: The Lorax | New |

Format: Microsoft PowerPoint docu... | ⬥ |

☐ Append file extension | Options... |

| Cancel | Save |

Figure 2.5   2001 Save Dialog Box

2. Type a file name in the *File Name* (**WIN 97 and 00**), *Name* (**MAC 01**), or *Save As* (**MAC 98**) box.

3. Click on the Navigation window at the top of the dialog box and find the location to which you would like to save your work. Possible locations include the desktop, a floppy, or in a folder.

4. Click **Save**.

✔**Troubleshooting Tip:** PowerPoint slide shows can be opened on both Windows and Macintosh computers if they are saved on a disk formatted for Windows. Be sure to add the extension ".ppt" to the end of the file name if you plan to transfer your slides to a PC.

👉 **Learn More:** Remember to save your work periodically by clicking on **File > Save** or clicking on the **Save** icon or by **Ctrl/⌘ + S**.

Applying a Design Template

Thus far, we have created a slide show on a blank white screen. It's time to add some flair to the slides by adding a template. A template contains a preset design with a color scheme, custom formatting, and fonts.

1. Select **Format** > **Apply Design** or **Apply Design Template** (WIN 00 & MAC 01) or the **Apply Design** icon. The *Apply Design Template* dialog box appears.

✔ **Troubleshooting Tip:** If the *Apply Design Template* dialog box does not appear, navigate to the Microsoft Office folder to locate them.

MAC 98: Microsoft Office 1998 folder > **Templates > Presentation Designs.**

MAC 01: Microsoft Office 2001 folder > **Templates > Presentations > Designs.**

2. Click on the different templates and view each example in the adjacent window. Double click on a template design to apply it to your slides.

✔ **Troubleshooting Tip:** If no design options are visible, you will need to locate the **Designs** folder. Click on the drop-down box at the top of the dialog box and first locate the **Microsoft Office** folder. In most cases, this is located on the hard drive. Then double click on the **Templates** folder. Next, double click on **Presentation Designs.**

MAC 01:   Select the **Presentations** folder
                     then the **Designs** folder.

☞ **Learn More:** Each version comes with a different set of templates. Most of the full slide pictures included in this book are from Windows 2000. Microsoft's Online Gallery has many free design templates available to download in their online Template Gallery. Go to officeupdate.microsoft.com/templategallery/ or navigate to the Web site from Microsoft's home page, www.microsoft.com/.

You can easily change your template anytime by repeating the same directions.

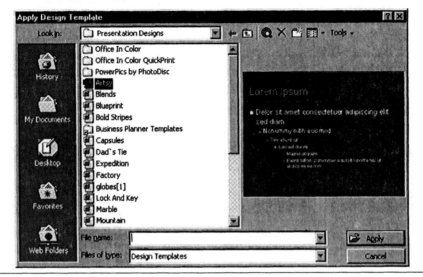

Figure 2.6   2000 Apply Design Dialog Box

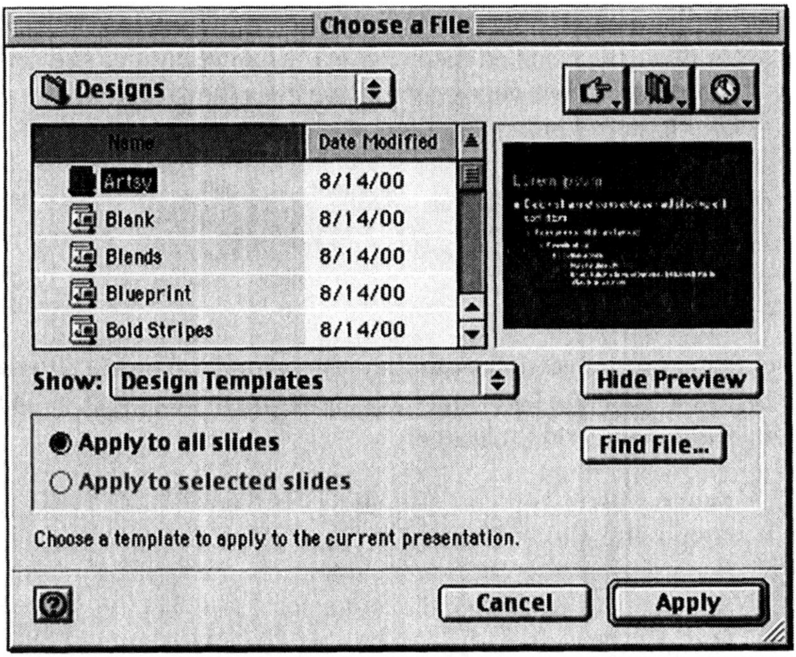

Figure 2.7   2001 Apply Design Dialog Box

Viewing Slides in Slide Sorter View

Click on the **Slide Sorter View** icon to view the four slides created thus far.

If your slides are not in this order, don't worry. Moving, deleting, and copying slides are covered in the next chapter.

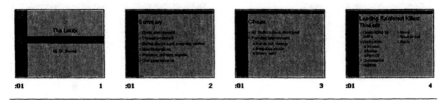

Figure 2.8   Four Slides in Slide Sorter View

Modifying Text

Changing font type, color, size, and alignment is quick and easy using the *Formatting* toolbar. Hold down the mouse while dragging the cursor across the text to be modified then release the mouse button. The text is now "highlighted." Now choose one of the tools shown below.

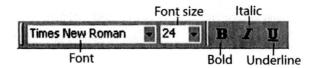

In the first two selections, use the *down* arrow to choose a different font style and size. The following tools allow you to modify the type by adding **Bold**, *Italic*, and <u>Underline</u>.

Learn More: You can also go to the menu at the top of the screen and choose **Format > Fonts**. Here you will find additional formatting options including changing the font color. Another way to change the font color is to select the **Font Color** icon. Fonts can be quickly replaced in a slide show by going to **Format > Replace Font**.

1. Use the sliding elevator button to the right of the screen to navigate to the title slide. Either hold down the button while sliding it to the top or click above the bar to move it up one slide at a time.

2. Highlight "The Lorax" and select a new font style, size, and color that also complement the template design.

3. Highlight "By Dr. Seuss" and italicize the text.

Modifying the Alignment

To instantly change the alignment of text, highlight it and select either the **Left, Center,** or **Right Alignment** icon.

Changing Bullets

To add or delete bullets on a slide, click on the **Bullets** icon. To change the bullet style, size, color, and/or indentation, go to **Format > Bullets/and Numbering.** (**WIN 97 & MAC 98** versions do not contain the numbering option.)

Check Your Work

Before closing the slide show, click on **Slide Sorter View** to observe the four slides created in this chapter.

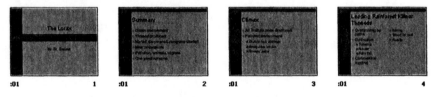

Save Changes and Exit

Click on the **Save** icon or **Ctrl/⌘ + S** to save your work. To exit PowerPoint, go to **File > Exit** or **Quit.**

WIN: Shortcut: Click on the **Close** button at the top right of the screen.

Or to exit the slide show while leaving PowerPoint open, go to **File >
Close.**

MAC: Shortcut: Click on the Close box on the top left of
                      the title bar.

Quick Review

▶ **Spell Check:**

Right click (MAC: Ctrl + Click) on misspelled word and select
correct spelling from drop-down menu.

▶ **Slide Panes and Slide Views:**

Outline Notes   Slide
                        Outline Sorter
Slide   Slide   Slide
         Sorter   Show   Normal Slide   Slide
                                                            Show

97/98 Views Labeled   00/01 Views Labeled

▶ **Work in Outline View:**

Promote Icon   01 Promote Icon

Demote Icon   01 Demote Icon

▶ **Create Slides in Normal or Slide View:**

Click on the Normal or Slide View icon

then press the New Slide icon

WIN 00:   Common Tasks > New Slide

▶ **Save a Slide Show:**

1. File > Save As.

2. Type a file name.

3. In the navigation window, select the location to save the slide show.

4. Click Save.

▶ **Apply a Design Template:**

Format > Apply Design or Apply Design Template **(WIN 00 & MAC 01)** or the Apply Design icon

▶ **Modify Text:**

Highlight text and then select one of the options below.

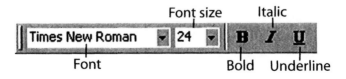

More options under: Format > Fonts

Font Color icon:

Modify Alignment:

► Change Bullets:

Bullets icon:

Format > Bullets/and Numbering.
To change the bullet style, size, color,
and/or indentation

► Save Changes and Exit:

Save icon

or Ctrl/⌘ + S

► Exit PowerPoint:

File > Exit or Quit
To exit the slide show while leaving PowerPoint open:
File > Close

3

Adding Graphs and Graphics

*I*n the last chapter, we created four slides and added a design template. Now, it is time to spice up the slides with a graph and add graphical elements.

Adding a Slide With a Graph

To illustrate how Dr. Seuss's book applies to the real world, we will create a graph illustrating the number of acres of rainforests destroyed each decade.

1. Open "The Lorax" slide show created in Chapter 2 by clicking on **File > Open** on the menu bar. The graph will be created in **Slide View** or in the **Slide Pane** window. The slide show will open up with the first slide, the Title.

This new slide will be created after the *Title Slide,* and will therefore become *Slide 2.*

2. From the **Slide Layout** dialog box, choose the **Chart** option, the last slide in the second row.

3. Title this slide by typing "Where have all the rainforests gone?"

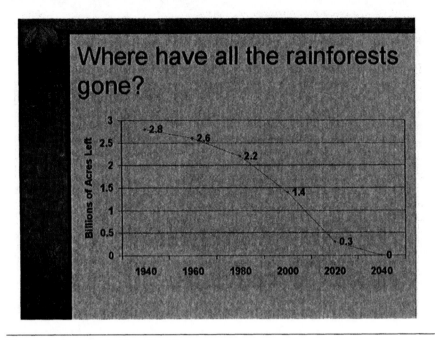

Figure 3.1   Basic Line Graph

4. Double click on the chart placeholder in the middle of the slide to add a chart. When the graph opens in PowerPoint, a data sheet (spreadsheet) and its corresponding chart/graph appear on the screen. (See Figure 3.2.)

5. To create a graph in PowerPoint, simply edit the information within the data sheet. Each rectangular box in the data sheet is called a cell and is named by the intersection of letters above and the column of numbers to the left. The first cell (first row, first column) is A1, the second cell in the first row is A2, and so forth. To the right and bottom of the data sheet are vertical and horizontal scroll bars that enable you to access more cells. Be careful to begin editing the cells with A1.

6. Click on the cell that reads "1st Qtr" and type "1940." Replace "2nd Qtr" with "1960," "3rd Qtr" with "1980," and continue through "2040." The **Tab** key moves the cursor forward from cell to cell. **Shift +Tab** moves the cursor back one cell. The arrow keys on the keyboard perform the same functions.

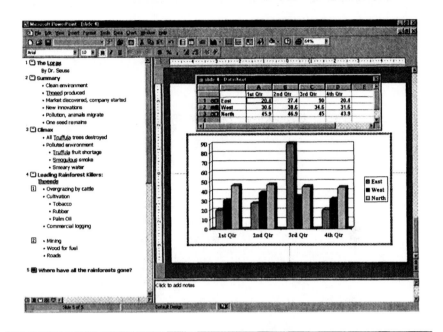

Figure 3.2   2000 Version (Initial Graph With Data Sheet)

7. Now remove rows 2 and 3. *Right* click (**MAC: Ctrl + Click**) on the number 2 cell and select **Delete** from the pop-up menu (on some versions, you may need to select **Entire row,** and **OK**). Repeat this process again to eliminate row 3.

8. *Right* click (**MAC: Ctrl + Click**) on the gray cell, top row, just before the A cell to bring up a drop-down menu and select **Clear Contents.** (This column is used to label the Legend or Key. This chart will not contain a legend because it has only one row of information.)

9. Replace the existing numbers in the PowerPoint table with the data provided below. For example, "2.8" should be placed in cell A1.

1940	1960	1980	2000	2020	2040
2.8	2.6	2.2	1.4	.3	0

Changing the Graph Type (Bar Graph to Line Graph)

1. Select **Chart > Chart Type** from the top menu to display the **Chart Type** dialog box.

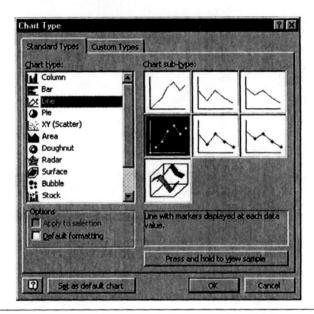

Figure 3.3   Chart Type Dialog Box

2. Under the **Standard Types** tab, select **Line** and click onto the line graph with the markers displayed at each data value (second row, first option), then **OK**.

☞ **Learn More: Chart Type** instantly converts one type of graph to another. Experiment by changing the graph into a pie chart, scatter chart, and so on.

Modifying a Graph

Next, modify the graph by adding value labels to each point, hiding the legend, and adding a graph title.

1. Select **Chart > Chart Options** from the menu to bring up the *Chart Options* dialog box.

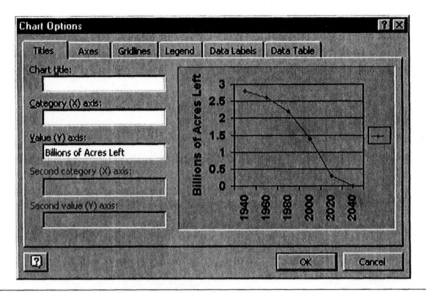

Figure 3.4   Chart Options Dialog Box

2. Choose the **Titles** tab and type "Billions of Acres Left" in the *Value (Y) axis* window.

3. Click on the **Legend** tab and deselect (uncheck) *Show Legend.*

4. In the **Data Labels** tab, click on *Show Value*, then **OK.**

Learn More: Modify nearly any feature on a graph by carefully *right* clicking (**MAC: Ctrl + Click**) on the feature and select editable options from the drop-down box.

5. Click anywhere off the data sheet and graph to return to the slide. To return to the data sheet to make changes to the graph, simply double click on the graph.

6. Click on the **Slide Sorter** at the bottom left of the screen to view in order the five slides created thus far.

If your slides are not in the same order, do not worry. Moving, deleting, and copying slides will be covered at the end of this chapter.

Remember to **Save** your work using the **Save Icon** or **Ctrl/⌘ + S.**

Adding Graphics

An easy method to add graphical elements to a slide is using a slide layout that includes a ClipArt placeholder.

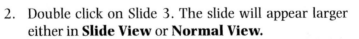

Figure 3.5   Summary Slide With Graphic

1. Navigate to Slide 3, titled "Summary," by selecting the **Slide Sorter View** icon

2. Double click on Slide 3. The slide will appear larger either in **Slide View** or **Normal View.**

3. Select **Format > Slide Layout** or click on the **Slide Layout** icon to bring up the *Slide Layout* dialog box.

4. Choose the "Text and ClipArt" slide (third row, first column) and click **Apply.** This layout will automatically place the text on the left side and automatically size graphics on the right. Click **Apply.**

5. Double click on the picture to bring up the Microsoft Gallery.

Using Microsoft's Gallery

Using the categories or typing in one or more words to search in the **Keyword** or **Search** windows are efficient ways to look for a specific graphic

✔ **Troubleshooting Tip:** If the Microsoft Gallery fails to appear, click the **Insert ClipArt** icon or select **Insert > Picture > ClipArt.**

☞ **Learn More:** The contents within Microsoft's Gallery vary with each version of PowerPoint. If the particular graphical examples shown in this book are not available in the Gallery, you might choose to find a similar substitute or look for it in Microsoft's online ClipArt gallery (explanation to follow).

WIN 97 & MAC 98

1. Click on the **Find** button on the right side of the Gallery box to open the *Find Clip* dialog box. (See Figure 3.6.)

2. In the **Keywords** window type "tree" and click on the **Find Now** button.

3. Double click on any ClipArt selection to insert it on the slide.

WIN 00

1. In the **Search for clips** window type "tree" and then press **Enter.** (See Figure 3.7.)

2. Click on a graphic to select it.

Locate a particular item by highlighting a category.

Use the **Find** button to quickly look up a particular graphic.

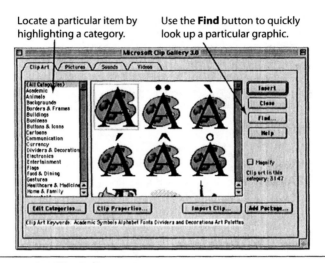

Figure 3.6 98 Clip Gallery

Click the **Back Arrow** to go to previous windows in MS Gallery or the **Forward Arrow** to return.

Click **All Categories** to bring back all categories after opening a file.

Quickly import graphics into the gallery or add graphics from Microsoft's Web site.

#1. Type "tree" in the Search for clips window.

Click once on any category in the main window to view all of the items in its field.

#2. Click once on a Clip Art picture to select it.

#3. Click once to insert the image onto a slide.

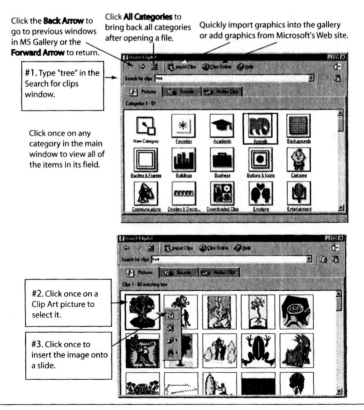

Figure 3.7 2000 MS Gallery

3. Click on the image again to bring up a drop-down menu.

4. Click on the **Insert Clip** icon (top icon) to insert the image on the slide.

MAC 01

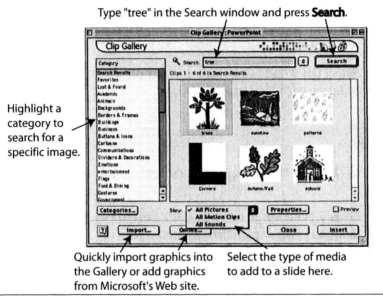

Type "tree" in the Search window and press **Search**.

Highlight a category to search for a specific image.

Quickly import graphics into the Gallery or add graphics from Microsoft's Web site.

Select the type of media to add to a slide here.

Figure 3.8   2001 MS Gallery

1. In the *Search* window, type "tree" and press **Return**.

2. Click on a graphic to select it and then click on **Insert** to place it on the slide.

Most graphics in the Gallery are classified under more than one name or category.

✓ **Troubleshooting Tip:** WIN 2000 and MAC 2001 versions support animated Gifs, whereas the older versions do not. To view motions or hear the added sounds, you will need to go to **Slide Show View**. Click on **Esc** to exit the view.

Accessing Microsoft's Design Gallery Live

PowerPoint contains a limited number of graphics, however, with an Internet connection, you can access Microsoft's large archive of downloadable graphics, sounds, and movies.

WIN 97

1. At the bottom right of the *Clip Gallery* window, select the button with the globe in it.

2. Select **OK** if the computer is already online. A browser will open to Microsoft's Design Gallery Live.

MAC 98

Accessing Microsoft's Design Gallery Live is not available for this version.

1. From a browser go to Microsoft's Design Gallery Live site at the following URL: dgl.microsoft.com.

2. In the *Search for* window, type "tree" and click **Go.**

3. The first of many pages of trees will appear on your screen.

4. Click and hold on the center of an image you wish to use.

5. In the drop-down menu, scroll down to the *Download image to disk* option.

6. Navigate to the location you wish to save the file and click **Save.**

7. Return to PowerPoint.

8. Select **Insert > Picture > From File** and locate the image. Click the **Insert** button.

WIN 00

1. Log on to the Internet.

2. Click the **Clips Online** icon in the ClipArt gallery. A browser will open to Microsoft's Design Gallery Live.

MAC 01

1. At the bottom of the *Clip Gallery* window, click the **Online** button.

2. When the *Launch Browser* dialog box asks if it is OK to launch the default Internet browser, choose *Yes*. A browser will open to Microsoft's Design Gallery Live.

To access the Design Gallery Live, users must choose *Accept* in regards to Microsoft's licensing agreement.

✔ **Troubleshooting Tip:** If Microsoft Clip Gallery Live fails to come up, open up a browser (such as Internet Explorer) and try again. If this fails, you can directly access Microsoft's online gallery by typing in its URL: cgl.microsoft.com/clipgallerylive/default.asp.

ALL VERSIONS

1. In the *Search for* window, type "tree" and press **Enter/Return.** Multiple pages of trees are available from which to choose.

2. After selecting the graphic(s) by checking the small box below the picture(s), a download click hyperlink will appear above the clips. Select it. A new Web page should appear.

3. Click on the **Download Now** link. The graphics are now archived in your ClipArt Gallery.

Customizing the Gallery

Categorize the downloaded graphics to quickly find them when needed.

1. *Right* click (**MAC: Ctrl + Click**) on the picture and select **Clip Properties** from the drop-down menu. The *Clip Properties* dialog box will appear. Select the **Categories** tab and check all of the categories under which the graphic could be classified.

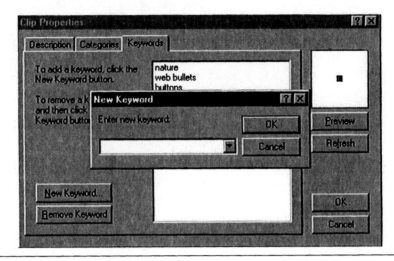

Figure 3.9   00 Clip Properties Dialog Box

✔**Troubleshooting Tip:** If you are working on MAC 98, capture the image from Microsoft's Design Gallery Live using the directions above. Select **Insert > Picture > ClipArt**. This brings up Microsoft's *ClipArt Gallery* dialog box. Click on the **Import Clip** button and navigate to the location of the captured image and click **Insert**. In the dialog box that appears, categorize the image and give it a keyword and click **OK**.

2. Go to the **Keyword** tab and click on the **New Keyword** button and type a keyword to quickly look up the ClipArt, then click **OK**. To make searches efficient, add a number of keywords that others might possibly use to search for this object.

Working With Graphics

1. Use **Slide Sorter View** to navigate to slide 4, titled "Climax."

2. Click on the **Slide Layout** icon and select the *Text* and *ClipArt* layout (first column, third row). The text will automatically be resized to fit into the left side of the slide.

3. Double click on the ClipArt placeholder and search for a picture of pollution or cut-down trees. Depending on the contents of

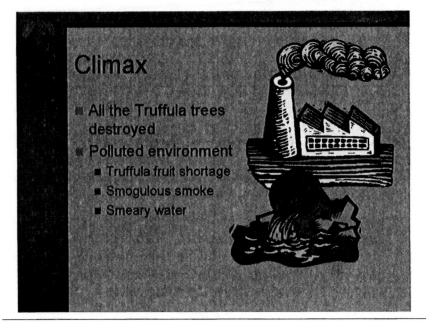

Figure 3.10 Climax Slide With Graphic

your ClipArt gallery, you may need to download pictures from Microsoft's Online Gallery. The ClipArt picture automatically resizes to fit the right side of the screen.

4. Add a second graphic to the right side. Click on the **Insert ClipArt** icon to bring up the ClipArt gallery and select a second picture to insert in the slide.

5. There are two graphics on the right side of the screen that need to be resized. Click on either of the images to select one. You will see eight small squares framing the object. These are the resizing handles.

6. Place the cursor over any of the resizing handles and the cursor will turn into a two-headed arrow. Press down on the resizing handles and drag the border inwards to reduce the image or outwards to enlarge the image. To avoid distorting the image (to retain the same proportion), press down and hold the **Shift** key and then drag one of the corner resizing handles.

Learn More: To create a circle or square, hold down **Shift** while dragging the corner resizing handles.

Troubleshooting Tip: An object must be selected to modify or edit it. If it is selected, it will be framed by several small squares.

7. To move the graphic to another location on the slide, make sure the graphic is selected. Put the cursor over the object until a four-headed arrow appears, then drag and drop (hold down the cursor on the object and drag) to the desired location.

8. **Overlapping images:** Move the objects until they are slightly overlapping. You can control which object is in the front and which is in the back. Place the bottom graphic in front of the top. Select the bottom graphic and select **Draw > Order** (bottom left of screen) and choose **Bring to Front**.

   MAC 01: Draw icon > Order

Learn More: Ordering (or Layering) Objects: When working with multiple overlapping objects, **Bring to Front** will place the object in front of all the objects. Likewise, **Bring to Back** will place it behind all of the objects. **Bring Forward** will place the object one layer forward and conversely, **Bring Backwards** will place the object one layer behind.

9. Go to Slide 5 by using the elevator bar to the left of **Normal** or **Slide View** or by locating it using **Slide Sorter View.** Add and resize an image like the example.

The Drawing Toolbar

Adding Slide 6

The conclusion slide illustrates the main point of the book: Individual actions do make a difference.

1. Click on the **New Slide** icon to create Slide 6. Choose the *Title Only* slide layout (third row, third column).

2. Type the title, "Conclusion and Analysis."

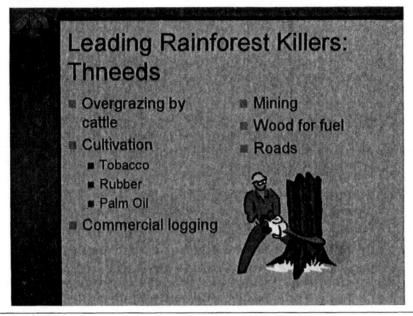

Figure 3.11   Leading Rainforest Killers Slide With Graphic

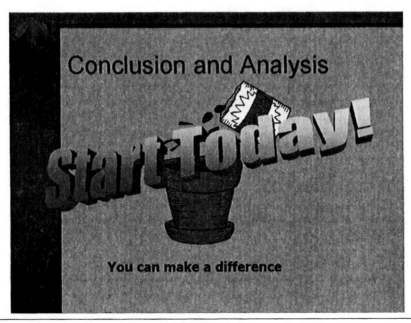

Figure 3.12   Conclusion Slide With Graphics

3. Insert a picture dealing with seeds or plants and position it in the center.

4. Add text to the bottom of the slide by creating a text box. On the *Drawing* toolbar select the **Text Box** icon. The cursor will turn into an upside down cross. Place the cross where you would like the text to begin and *right* click on the mouse. A small rectangular text box will form and enlarges as you type. In the text box, type "You can make a difference."

5. While the textbox is still selected, select **Draw > Align or Distribute** and select **Relative to Slide**. Select **Draw > Align or Distribute** again and select **Align Center** from the menu to center the text box automatically on the slide.

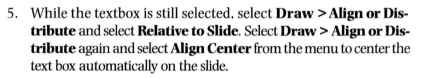 **Learn More:** The **Align and Distribute** tool is useful for positioning one or more objects perfectly on a slide. To select more than one object, hold down **Shift** while clicking on each object.

Adding WordArt

1. Click on the **WordArt** icon on the *Drawing* toolbar. The *WordArt Gallery* dialog box will appear with many design options. Select an option that is not angled and click **OK**.

2. A new dialog box will appear labeled *Edit WordArt Text*. In the window under *Text*, you will see the words "Your Text Here." Replace those words with "Start Today!"

3. Change the font size to 54 using the downward arrow under *Size*, then click **OK**.

4. Drag and place the WordArt to the desired position on the slide.

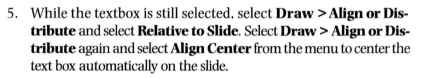 **Learn More:** For more WordArt options, use the **WordArt** toolbar. The toolbar may automatically appear when WordArt is selected. If it does not appear, select **View > Tools > WordArt**. Modify and edit the WordArt in a variety of ways with each icon on the toolbar. Try out each of the functions.

Rotating WordArt

1. Make sure **WordArt** is selected on the slide. Click on the **Free Rotate** icon on the **Drawing** toolbar or on the floating **WordArt** toolbar. Four small green circles will border the graphic. When the cursor is held over one of these green circles, it will turn into a circular arrow.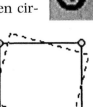

2. Press and hold the cursor down on one of the circular arrows and turn it in the desired direction, then release the mouse button.

✔ **Rotating ClipArt Tip:** If the **Free Rotate** icon will not work with ClipArt, try grouping and ungrouping it first. Select the object and select **Draw > Ungroup**. While the object is still selected, go back to **Draw** and select **Group**. Now try the **Free Rotate** icon once again.

MAC 01:   > Ungroup

Adding Shapes

1. Navigate to the first slide, the Title slide.

Figure 3.13. Title Slide With Graphic

2. Add a starburst to the title slide by clicking and pressing on the *down* arrow next to **AutoShapes** on the **Drawing** toolbar and choose **Stars and Banners**. Choose a starburst, such as *Explosion 2*. The cursor will turn into crosshairs (or plus sign).

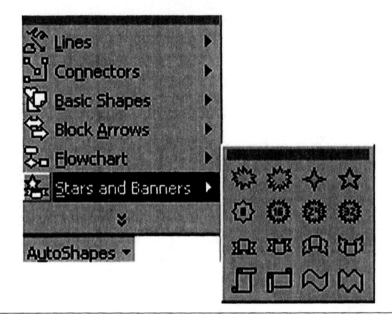

Figure 3.14 AutoShapes Starburst

MAC 01:   **Draw** icon **> Stars and Banners**

3. Place the crosshairs to position the starburst. While holding down the mouse button, drag it across the screen. A starburst will appear.

4. Make the starburst larger or smaller by placing the selection arrow over the small squares framing the starburst (the cursor will turn into a two-headed arrow) then hold the cursor down and drag it to the desired size.

Modifying the Starburst

1. Change the fill color of the starburst by clicking on the down arrow next to the **Fill Color** icon. Selecting *No Fill* will make the

starburst transparent. *Automatic* will color the object using a default color that normally complements the chosen template. *More Colors* will bring up the *Custom* and *Standard Color Palettes* for a broader color selection. Choose **Fill Effects** to fill the object with a gradient, texture, pattern, or a picture.

2. Make the starburst three-dimensional by clicking on the **3D** icon and select a 3D option. Clicking on the 3D setting will bring up the **3-D Settings** toolbar, giving options to customize the three-dimensional characteristics of the object.

Learn More: The **Shadow** icon will create a shadow for an object. Normally you cannot add both a shadow and 3D effect to an object.

3. Click on the starburst and type "Save the Trees." Depending on the size of the starburst, the text may not fit inside. With the starburst still selected, go to **Format > AutoShape** and choose the **Text Box** tab. Click on *Resize Autoshape to fit text,* then **OK.**

Grouping a Text Box and Arrow

1. Navigate to Slide 2, the Line Graph.

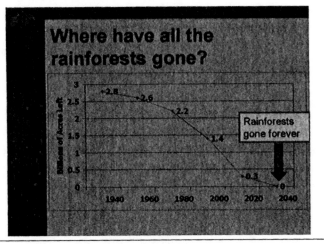

Figure 3.15 Line Graph Slide With Graphic

2. Click on the **Rectangular** icon to turn the cursor into cross-hairs (or plus sign).

3. Position the crosshairs to insert a rectangle, then hold down and drag the rectangle to the desired size.

4. With the rectangle still selected, type "Rainforests gone forever."

5. Change the fill color with the rectangle still selected, by clicking on the **Fill Color** icon.

6. Add a thicker perimeter to the rectangle by selecting the **Line Style** icon and choose *3 pt.* for the line thickness.

7. Change the color of the border of the rectangle by choosing the down arrow next to the **Line Color** icon. (No line will eliminate the border or perimeter around the object.)

8. Click on **AutoShapes > Block arrow** and choose the *down* arrow. Resize the arrow to fit the rectangle and place it just below the rectangle (see Figure 3.14).

MAC 01: **> Block Arrows**

9. To perfectly align the rectangle and the arrow, select both objects while holding down the Shift key. Select **Draw > Align and Distribute** and choose **Align Center**.

MAC 01: **> Align and Distribute**

10. With the two objects still selected, combine them to form one object. This is called Grouping. Select **Draw** or the icon to the right and select *Group*. The object will now move as one object.

11. Move the arrow so that it is positioned just above the point where the line graph dips to 0.

Moving, Deleting, and Copying in Slide Sorter View

There are two primary ways to move slides in **Slide Sorter View:** the **Drag and Drop** and **Cut and Paste** Methods.

Move Slide 2, the Line Graph, behind Slide 5, titled "Leading Rainforest Killers: Thneeds" by clicking on the **Slide Sorter** icon.

Drag and Drop Method

1. Click on Slide 2, the Line Graph. The border around the slide will darken.

2. Hold down the mouse and drag Slide 2 to the right of the "Leading Rainforest Killers" slide. A vertical line will appear between Slides 5 and 6.

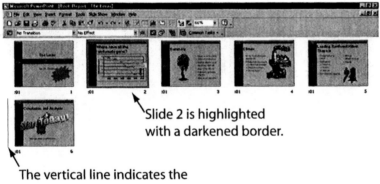

Slide 2 is highlighted
with a darkened border.

The vertical line indicates the
new location for Slide 2.

3. Release the mouse. The line graph is now the fifth slide in the presentation.

Cut and Paste Method

The **Cut** icon will take the text or object (or entire slide in **Slide Sorter View**) selected and place it on a clipboard that you cannot see, ready to paste where you wish.

Cut Copy Paste

The **Copy** icon does not eliminate the text or object (or slide in **Slide Sorter View**) selected. It makes a copy of it on the clipboard. Select **Paste** to insert the cut or copied object, text or slide to a new location.

1. Highlight Slide 2, the Line Graph.

2. Click on the **Cut** icon. Slide 2 will disappear and the slides consequently are renumbered.

3. Click in the space to the right of the slide labeled, "Leading Rainforest Killers: Thneeds." A vertical line will appear between Slides 4 and 5.

4. Select the **Paste** icon to insert the Line Graph behind the "Leading Rainforest Killers" slide.

Arrange the six slides in the following order for animations in the next chapter.

Figure 3.16   Final Slides 1 Through 3

Figure 3.17   Final Slides 4 Through 6

Quick Review

▶ **Working With Graphs:**

Tab: Moves cursor forward from cell to cell

Shift + Tab: Moves cursor back one cell

Change type
of graph: Chart > Chart Type

Modify graph: Chart > Chart Options or *Right* click
(MAC: Ctrl + Click) onto an element
on the graph

▶ **Adding Graphics:**

Insert > Picture > ClipArt or
click on the Insert ClipArt icon

Microsoft's Clip Gallery Live
cgl.microsoft.com/clipgallerylive/default.asp

▶ **Customizing Microsoft Gallery:**

Right click (MAC: Ctrl + Click) on graphic >
Clip Properties > Categories and Keyword tab

▶ **Important Tools and Toolbars:**

Cut   Copy   Paste

Drawing Toolbar

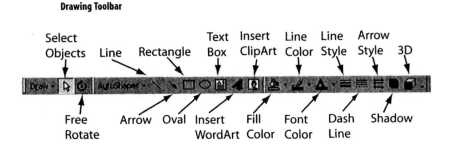

Select   Text   Insert   Line   Line   Arrow
Objects   Line   Rectangle   Box   ClipArt   Color   Style   Style   3D

Free   Arrow   Oval   Insert   Fill   Font   Dash   Shadow
Rotate   WordArt   Color   Color   Line

Drawing Menu

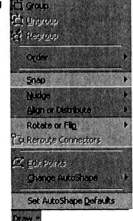

AutoShapes Menu

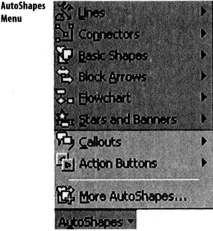

2001 Drawing Toolbar

Draw

Select Objects

Free Rotate

Text Box

Insert WordArt

Insert ClipArt

Insert Picture from File

Line

Rectangle

AutoShapes

Lines

Line Style

Font Color

Line Color

Fill Color

Shadow
3D

2001 Drawing Menu

2001 AutoShapes Menu

Special Effects

When building a slide show, animation effects can add a bit of magic to any presentation. Two major ways to integrate these special effects are through instant animations or custom animations. The first, instant animations, can be accessed through the **Animation Effects** toolbar. The second, custom animations, can add even more options to spice up a presentation. It is located at **Slide Show > Custom Animation (MAC 01: Slide Show > Custom > Animation)**.

Adding Instant Animation Effects

1. Navigate to the title slide.

2. Click on the **Animation Effects** icon to bring up the Animation Effects toolbar or click on **View > Toolbars > Animation Effects**.

3. Select the starburst object ("Save the Trees").

4. Select the **Camera Effect** icon on the *Animation Effects* toolbar. Notice that many of the animation effects icons turned from gray to colored. These icons are the effects that can be applied to the starburst.

5. Select the title on the slide.

6. Select **Slide Show > Preset Animation** (MAC 01: **Slide Show > Animations**). Select *Dissolve* to animate the title with that effect.

Each version of PowerPoint has a slightly different Animation Effects toolbar. However, all versions have the following 10 instant effects, ordered from left to right. Nonnumbered effects apply only to the version(s) listed. Note that all these effects are available in all versions via Custom Animation.

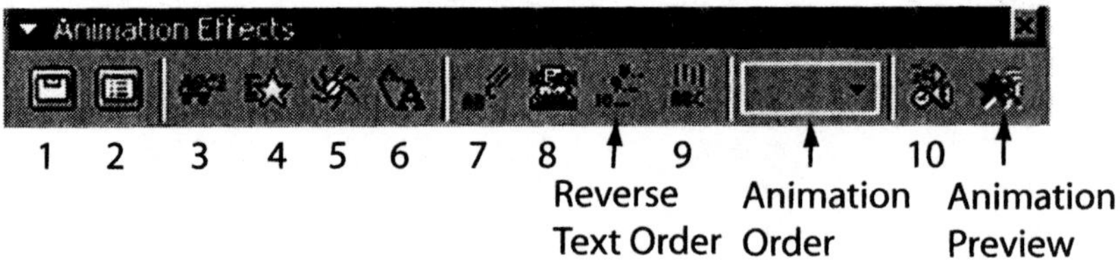

Figure 4.1   2000 Animation Effects Toolbar

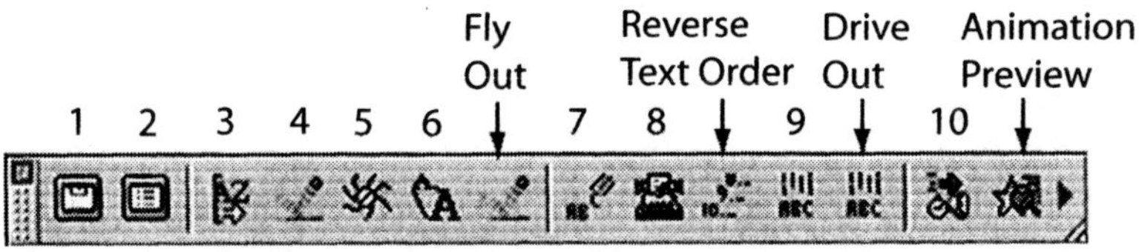

Figure 4.2   2001 Animation Effects Toolbar

1. **Animate Title:** Animates the slide title automatically without having to select it.

2. **Animate Slide Text:** Animates the text on the slide.

3. **Drive-In Effect:** Brings in object/text from the right with a "vroom" sound.
   - **MAC 01:** Drive-In/Out: After object/text drives in from the right, it drives off the left side of the screen.

4. **Flying or Fly In:** Brings object/text in from the left with a "whoosh" sound.

5. **Camera:** Makes object/text appear from the center outward with a camera-like noise.

6. **Flash Once:** Flashes the object/text on the screen once, disappearing afterwards.
   - **Fly Out:** Sends the object/text off the right side of the screen with a "whoosh" sound.

7. **Laser Text:** Object/text comes in from the left corner of the screen with a redundant "Star Wars Laser" sound. Text appears one letter at a time.

8. **Typewriter Text:** Text comes in one letter at a time from the left with a "typing" noise.
   - **Reverse Text Order:** Reverses the animation order of the text. (All versions except MAC 2001.)

9. **Drop In:** The text/object drops in from the top center of the screen. Text appears one word at a time.
   - **Drop Out (MAC 01):** Makes text/object drop out to the bottom of the screen.
   - **Animation Order Box:** Change the order in which the animations occur if there is more than one object or item on the slide. (All versions except MAC 2001.)

10. **Custom Animation:** Opens the Custom Animation dialog box that allows even more control and options for controlling animations, timings, and sounds.
   - **Animation Preview (WIN 00 & MAC 01):** View animations without going into Slide Show View.

Drive-In, Flying, Camera, Flash Once, Typewriter, and Drop In Effects are also available from the menu by going to **Slide Show > Preset Animation (MAC 01: Slide Show > Animations). Wipe Right, Dissolve, Split Vertical Out**, and **Appear** are instant animation options available from the menu but are not on the Animation Effects toolbar.

Viewing Animation Effects

The most efficient method to view how these effects will look in the actual slide show is to view them in the Preview window.

WIN 00 & MAC 01:   Select the **Animation Preview** icon at the end of the *Animation Effects* toolbar.

WIN 97 & MAC 98:   Select the **Custom Animation** icon at the end of the toolbar. Then select the **Preview** button on the right side of the preview screen.

Another way to view the animations is in **Slide Show View**. Press the **Enter/Return** key, the **Space Bar,** or click on the mouse button to view each added effect. To exit Slide Show View press **Esc** on the keyboard.

Preset animations are quick and easy to use, however, they do not meet the needs of all presentations. The reoccurring and redundant sound effects can annoy and distract an audience. Use them judiciously.

Adding Custom Animation Effects

Custom animation effects allows for many more options and specific control of animation effects.

1. Navigate to the second slide ("Summary Slide") and make sure to be in **Normal** or **Slide View**.

2. Select the **Custom Animation** icon on the *Animation toolbar* or select **Slide Show > Custom Animation (MAC 01: Slide Show > Custom > Animation)**. The Custom Animation dialog box will appear.

3. Make sure the **Order and Timing (WIN 97 & MAC 98: Timing)** tab is selected.

4. Select Title 1, Text 2 (bulleted text), and Object 3 (tree) for animation by using the following directions for each of the versions.

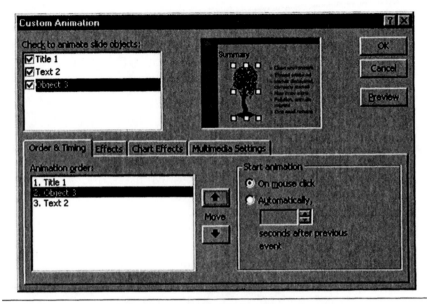

Figure 4.3   2000 Custom Animation Dialog Box

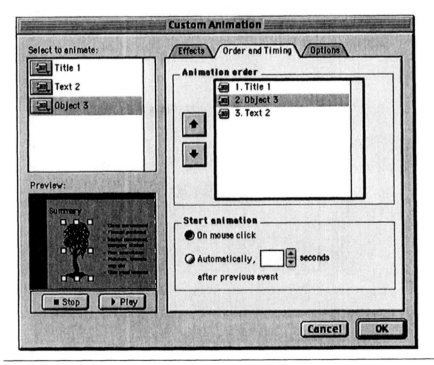

Figure 4.4   2001 Custom Animation Dialog Box

WIN 97 & MAC 98:   Click once on Title 1 in the timing window and then select the **Animate** button to the right. Do the same thing for Text 2 and Object 3.

WIN 00:   Check the boxes next to Title 1, Text 2, and Object 3 to select them for animation.

MAC 01:   Click on the icon to the left of Title 1 to see a drop-down list of options. Choose *Entry* to animate the entry of the text. Do the same for Text 2 and Object 3.

5. Title 1, Text 2, and Object 3 are now listed in the *Animation Order* window. Change the order of the animations by using the *up* and *down* arrows. Select an object in the *Animation Order* window and move it one place forward in the animation order with a click of the *up* arrow or one position backwards with the *down* arrow. Make sure the order is Title 1, Object 3, and Text 2.

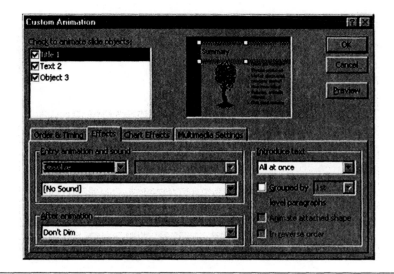

Figure 4.5   Animation Effects

6. Select the **Effects** tab. Highlight Title 1 in the window in the upper left. Under *Entry animation and sound* choose *Dissolve* in the first drop-down window.

7. Highlight Object 3 (tree) in the window in the upper left. Select the animation *Stretch from Bottom* to make the tree to appear to grow.

   WIN 00:   Choose *Stretch* in the first window and *From Bottom* in the second window.

8. Highlight Text 2. Under *Entry animation and sound* choose *Wipe Right* in the first drop-down window.

   WIN 00:   Select *Wipe* in the first window and *Right* in the next window.

   MAC 01:   Choose *Wipe* and then scroll over and choose *Right*.

9. The *Introduce Text* window allows you to choose whether you wish the text to come in one letter at a time, one word at a time, or all at once. Choose *All at once.* Check the box next to *Grouped by* and select *1st* level paragraphs.

   MAC 01:   Click on the **Options** tab to view the *Text entry options* and choose *All at once,* with bullets grouped by *2nd level.* Select the **Effects** tab again.

Learn More: Grouping by 1st level animates all the text under each bulleted topic all at once. Grouping by 2nd animates each bulleted topic, followed by all text in the 2nd or subtopic level.

10. In the *After Animation* window, choose a color that contrasts with the main text of the slide. Selecting *More Colors* provides more color options from a color palette. When each new line of bulleted text animates across the screen, the previous bulleted text changes to another color. Ideally, the text will appear to dim, yet still be readable. The audience will now be directed to follow the new point but can still read the more dim previous points.

Learn More: Make sure the color selected is visible against the template background. A good rule of thumb is to use light text on a dark background or dark text on a light background. The default colors at the top of the palette tend to complement the design if you are using one of Microsoft's templates.

11. Click on the **Preview** button (**MAC 01: Play** button) to see what these animations will look like in the preview window. When satisfied click on **OK**.

The first two slides have been animated with instant and custom animation effects. (See Table 4.1.)

Add the animation effects in Table 4.1 to Slides 3 through 6 in the listed order.

Directions for Animating the Line Graph on Slide 5

On Slide 5, the title should first dissolve. Second, the graph appears to grow across the screen. Finally, a sound effect will sound as the sign "Rainforests gone forever" animates from the top of the screen to point to the end of the line graph.

1. In **Custom Animation**, animate the title and choose the *Dissolve* effect.

2. Under the **Order and Timing** tab, select the *Chart* and *Grouped Object* for animation.

3. Highlight the Chart 1 in the upper left-hand window. Choose the **Chart Effects** tab. Select *Introduce chart* elements *by Category*. Deselect the check box next to *Animate grid and legend*. Under *Entry animation and sound* choose *Wipe Right*. (See Figure 4.5.)

   MAC 01: Select the **Effects** tab. Choose *Wipe Right*. Select the **Options** tab. Select *Introduce chart* elements *by Category*. Deselect the check box next to *Animate grid and legend*.

4. Highlight Group 3 in the upper left window.

Table 4.1

Slide # and Title	Animation effects for each slide in the "correct" animation order
1. The Lorax	Title: Dissolve Starburst (with text): Camera Effect
2. Summary	Tree (Object): Stretch from Bottom Bulleted Text: Wipe Right; All at once; Dim to a contrasting color
3. Climax	Title: Dissolve Objects: Checkerboard Down Bulleted Text: Wipe Right, Introduce text (MAC 01: Text entry options) All at once; grouped by 2nd Level; Dim to the same contrasting color as slide 2.
4. Leading . . .	Title: Dissolve Object: Box In Bulleted Text: Wipe Right; Introduce text (MAC 01: Text entry options) All at once; Grouped by 2nd Level; Dim to the same contrasting color as slide 2.
5. Where . . .	Title: Dissolve Chart: Wipe Right. *Do not* animate grid and legend. Grouped Object: Fly From Top Right with explosion or laser sound.
6. Conclusion	Seed Picture: No animation Title: Dissolve Text Box: Zoom In Word Art: Swivel

5. Under the **Effects** tab, choose *Fly (In) From Top-Right*. Directly underneath this drop-down box is the sound box. Choose *Explosion* or *Laser.*

6. Preview the animations using the **Preview** button and then click **OK**.

Troubleshooting Tip: Animation effects should enhance the readability of your text.

- Save the *introduce text by letter* and *word* options for titles and headings.

- Animation effects for the main text of a slide should not appear "choppy" to the audience. Waiting for text to appear one word at a time is irritating. Conversely, text that disappears before the audience can read it can be frustrating.

- Animate the titles and text in a fairly consistent manner. The inclusion of too many effects is one of the most common mistakes of PowerPoint users. After finishing your slide show, try to view your project objectively to determine if it enhances your slides and message. Special effects can be distracting and annoying to an audience.

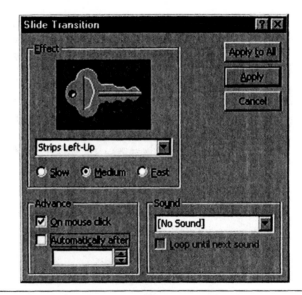

Figure 4.6   Slide Transition Dialog Box

Adding Transitions

An animation assigns movement to objects or text on a slide; a transition determines how the slide will change when it advances to the next slide.

1. Select **Slide Show > Slide Transition** to bring up the *Slide Transition* dialog box. (See Figure 4.6.)

   The picture of a key (or, in WIN 97, a dog) in the top window represents the slides in "The Lorax." Use the *down* arrow under the key to experiment with different transition effects. Control how quickly one slide will move to the next by selecting *Slow, Medium,* or *Fast.*

2. Under *Advance* choose *On mouse click* to make each slide advances forward with the click of the spacebar or mouse. Notice the option that allows slides to advance automatically by selecting *Automatically after . . .* then choose the number of seconds. In addition, sound effects can be added with transitions, but be aware, too many sound effects can be distracting.

3. Apply the *Strips Left-Up* transition effect at *Medium* speed to all slides at once by selecting the **Apply to All** button. The **Apply** button just uses the selected transition on the current slide.

In **Slide Sorter View**, a small slide graphic on the bottom left corner of each slide means that a transition effect has been assigned to the slide.  When using the advance timer to have slides transition automatically, a number will appear next to this symbol illustrating the number of seconds it will take to advance to the next slide.

View these transition effects in the *Custom Animation Preview* window or in **Slide Show View**.

Using Automatic Timers

Slide Transitions are just one way to set up automatic timers on a slide. For more specific control over individual objects or text in a show,

1. Select the *Custom Animation* dialog box and select the **Order** or the **Order and Timing** tab.

2. Select any animated object. Select the button next to *Automatically* under *Start animation* and use the *up/down* arrows to choose the number of seconds to elapse before the show will begin the selected animation. This can be done for each animation in a show. For example, someone presenting material from the "Climax" slide of "The Lorax" show, might want to have one of the graphics automatically come in when that third slide begins. Then, they might want to talk about that graphic for 10 or 15 seconds before the next graphic appears.

Troubleshooting Tip: If automatic timings do not work when you view them in **Slide Show View**, select **Slide Show > Set Up Show**. Make sure *Advance slides using timings if present* is chosen in the dialog box. Conversely, you can show your slides with a click of a mouse or keyboard without deleting your slide timings by selecting *Advance Slides Manually.*

Quick Review

▶ **Instant Animation Effects:**

Animation Effects icon or View > Toolbars > Animation Effects or Slide Show > Preset Animations

▶ **Custom Animation Effects:**

Slide Show > Custom Animation (MAC 01: Slide Show > Custom > Animation)

Slide Show > Preset Animation (MAC 01: Slide Show > Animations)

Custom Animation icon
1. Timing (and Order) Tab: Select items to animate, choose animation order, automatic or manual timings
2. Effects Tab: Select animation and sound effects
3. Chart Effects tab: Use to animate graphs

▶ **View Animation Effects:**

Click on Slide Show View

WIN 00 & MAC 01:   Animation Preview icon

WIN 97 & MAC 98:   Custom Animation icon >
Preview

▶ **Transition Effects:**

Slide Show > Slide Transition

5

Presentation Delivery

PowerPoint offers many tools that allow presenters to maximize the impact of a presentation. From printing out handouts and speaker notes, to using a pen tool to highlight information, this software is focused on presentation.

Adding Speaker's Notes

The Lorax slide show is almost finished. The only thing remaining is to complete the final preparations that can improve how the material is presented. Slide 4 is a segue slide that transitions from the book to real life. The "thneeds" were the killers of the Lorax trees. The bulleted text highlights modern day "thneeds" that are killing our rainforests. There is a lot of information about each of these bullets that needs to be mentioned. This information will be added to the speaker's notes for that slide.

1. **WIN 00 & MAC 01:** Navigate to the 4th slide and enlarge the *Notes* pane. Click in the *Notes* pane to begin adding notes. If the area just below the *Slide* pane does not state "Click to add notes," the pane may be buried at the bottom of the *Slide View*. Move the cursor down to the bottom of the screen until it changes to a two-headed arrow. Click and drag the pane up as far as it will go.

WIN 97 & MAC 98: Navigate to the 4th slide and switch to Notes Page View. Use the Zoom drop-down menu on the *Standard* toolbar to enlarge the *Notes* view. Click in the *Notes* pane to begin adding text.

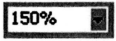

2. Change the font size to at least 20.

3. Type in the following main points needed for the presentation.

   • Since the Central American cattle boom, more than 25% of the area's rainforests have been cleared.

   • Only one tree is planted for every ten cut in most tropical countries.

   • Approximately 2,000 trees per minute are cut down. (Source: www.rainforestlive.org.uk/)

4. **Save** the slide show.

5. To use these notes while delivering the slides, it is necessary to print them using the **Notes Pages** or **Outline View** options in the *Print* dialog box shown in Figure 5.3. Speaker's notes are not visible on the screen when presenting the slide show in **Slide Show View.**

Printing

Printing Speaker's Notes

There is only one page of speaker's notes that were typed for this presentation (Slide 4). Print this page of speaker's notes to use as an aid in presenting this material.

1. Select **File > Print.**

2. Select the slides you wish to copy under *Print Range* (**MAC 98 & 01:** *Pages*).

   WIN 97 & 00: Click on the button next to *Slides.* Type "4" in the window.

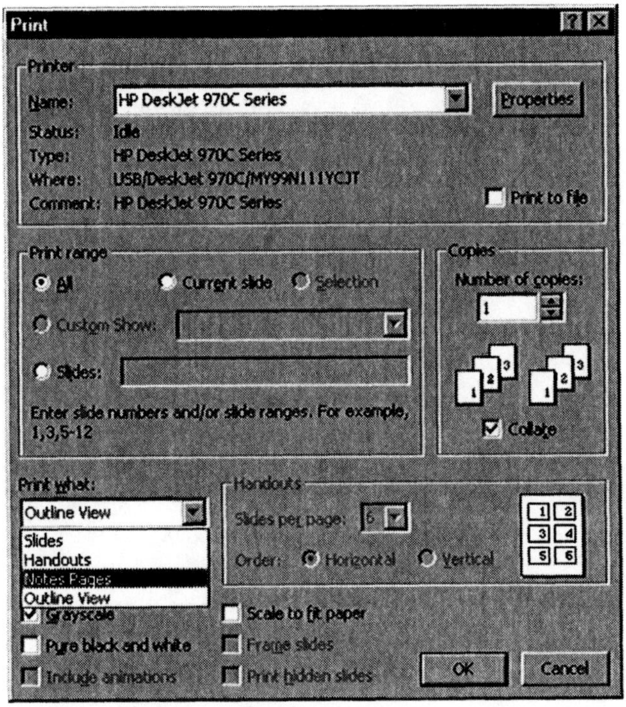

Figure 5.1   2000 Print Dialog Box

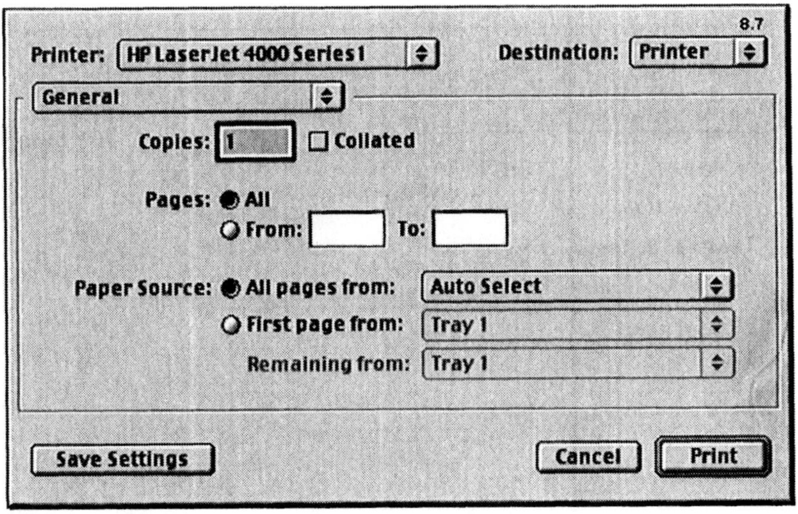

Figure 5.2   Mac Print Dialog Box

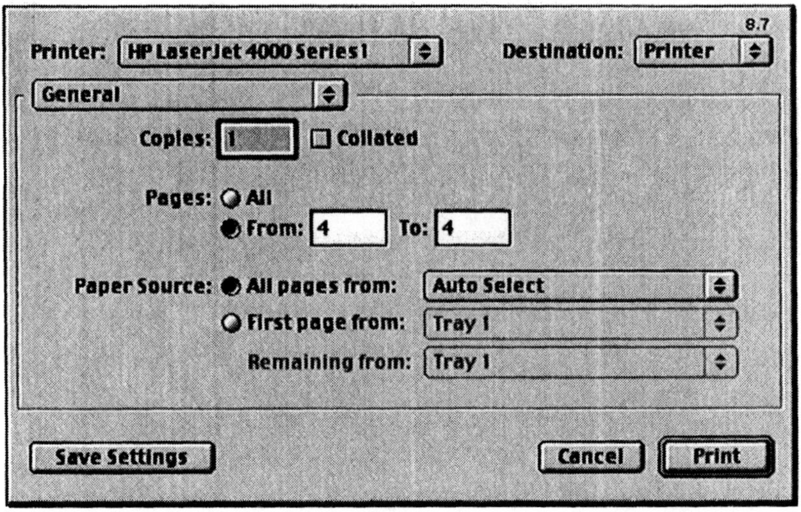

Figure 5.3   Mac Print Dialog Box (4 and 4)

MAC 98 & 01:   Click on the button next to *From:* and type "4" and "4." (See Figure 5.3.) In the drop-down box in the top left, change *General* to *Microsoft PowerPoint.*

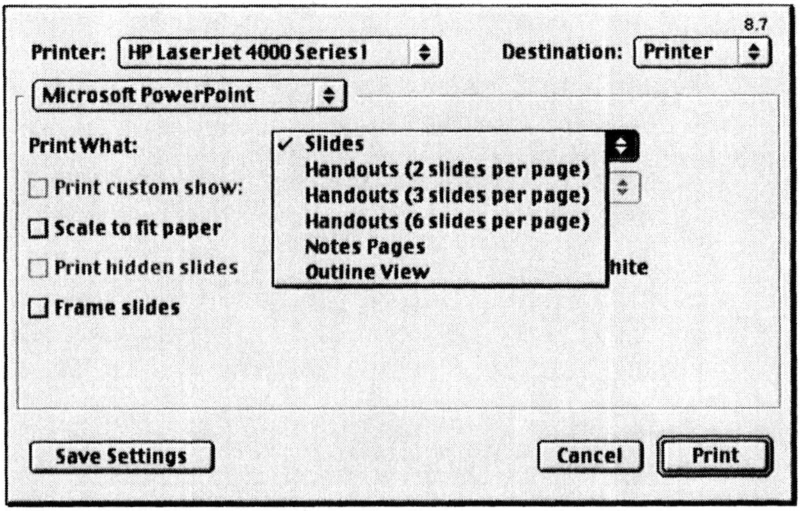

Figure 5.4   Mac PowerPoint Print Dialog Box

3. Under *Print What* use the *down* arrow to select *Notes Pages.*

4. Click **OK** (**MAC 98 & 01: Print**).

Printing Handouts

Students will need to take notes on this presentation. Use the three slides per page to print note-taking handout for students.

1. Select **File > Print.**

2. Choose the slides you wish to print. Select the **All** button under *Print Range.*

   MAC 98 & 01:   Select the **All** button next to *Pages.* In the drop-down box in the top left, change *General* to *Microsoft PowerPoint.*

3. Under *Print What* choose *Handouts* (3 slides per page).

   WIN 00:   Under *Print What* choose *Handouts.* Under *Slides Per Page* choose 3.

✔ **Troubleshooting Tip:** To save your color print cartridges, check *Gray Scale* or *Black and White* at the bottom of the *Print* dialog box.

4. Select **OK** (**MAC 98 & 01: Print**).

Other Printing Options

► **Slides:** Prints one slide per page. Useful for class posters or transparencies.

► **Handouts:** Prints several slides on one page. Choose to print 2, 3, 4, or 6 slides per page (**WIN 00:** 9 slides per page are available).

► **Notes Pages:** Prints one slide on each page with speaker's notes at the bottom. This option may be useful for providing students with a printed overview or a review sheet of a lesson.

► **Outline View:** Prints slides in outline form. Titles and text only are visible.

✔**Troubleshooting Tip:** Caution: Pressing the **Print** icon on the *Standard* toolbar will print full pages of each slide. It does not provide any print options.

Final Preparation for Presenting

One idea for presenting this material is to switch to the pen mode (mouse pen) when you reach your final slide. In red, underline "Start Today." Now, switch to a blank white or black screen to reflect with the students as they brainstorm ways to save the rainforest. Finally, return to the presentation, erase the red line, and then circle the word "You" a few times for emphasis.

1. Before starting the slide show, go to **Slide Show > Set Up Show**, and choose a red color in *Pen Color.*

2. Navigate to the first slide and begin presenting the slides in slide show mode by selecting **Slide Show > View Show** or clicking on the **Slide Show View** icon.

3. After the final sentence animates on the last slide, shift to pen mode by selecting **Ctrl/⌘ + P.** The arrow cursor changes to a pen.

4. Underline "Start Today" a few times.

5. Circle the word "You" a few times for emphasis.

6. Select **E** on the keyboard to erase the underline.

7. Select the **W** (or **B**) key to change the screen to white (or black). Brainstorm ways students can help to save the rainforest. (Note: Changing the screen to white or black will erase any markings added with the pen tool.)

8. Select the **W** (or **B**) key again to return to the slide show.

9. To switch from pen mode back to arrow mode, select **Ctrl/⌘ + A.**

Presentation Keyboard Commands

► **Esc: ESC**ape or exit Slide Show View

▶ **P:** Select Previous Slide or Previous Animation

▶ To go to a particular slide, enter the slide number on the keyboard and then press **Enter/Return**. For example, if a student wanted to see the 4th slide again ("Leading Rainforest Killers"), simply press "4" and **Enter/Return**.

Quick Review

▶ **Adding Speaker's Notes:**

WIN 97 & MAC 98:   Use Notes Pages

WIN 00 & MAC 01:   Use Notes Pane

Print Speaker's Notes: Select Notes Pages or Outline View options in the Print dialog box

▶ **Printing:**

Select File > Print

1. Select the slides under *Print Range* (**MAC 98 & 01:** *Pages*).

   MAC 98 & 01: Change General to Microsoft PowerPoint.

2. Under "Print What" select Slides, Handouts, Notes Pages, or Outline View.

3. Check Gray Scale or Black and White to save colored ink.

▶ **Presentation Shortcuts:**

Keyboard Commands	Function
Esc	Escape
N	Next slide
Enter	Next slide
P	Previous slide
W	White screen
B	Blank screen
E	Erase pen marks
5 + Enter/Return	Skip to Slide 5
Ctrl/⌘ + P	Shift to Pen
Ctrl/⌘ + A	Shift to Arrow

6

Classroom Applications

Develop a Custom School Template

Use the Slide Master to create a consistent template for all slides in official school presentations, complete with school colors and mascot or logo. Changes made to the background, color scheme, fonts, text alignment, and bullets on the Slide Master are applied to every slide. Placing a graphic of the school mascot/logo on the Slide Master places that graphic in the same place on every slide. Without the Slide Master, the graphic would have to be added separately to each slide. Using the Slide Master would also be the best way to change bullets in a presentation so that the main points have a particular type of star, the subpoints begin with a square, and so forth. When finished with the Slide Master, all slides in the slide show will include the newly created template.

Adding a Gradient Background With School Colors

Gradients are gradual color transitions using two or more colors. Gradient techniques add the illusion of depth to slides.

1. Switch to the slide master in **View > Master > Slide Master**.

2. Add a background color scheme. Select **Format > Background** to bring up the *Background* dialog box.

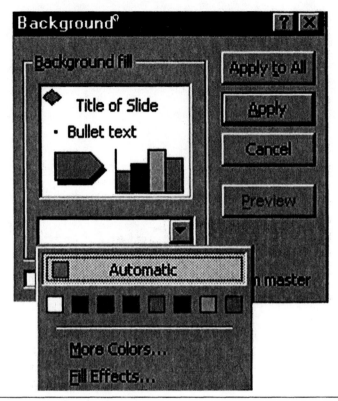

Figure 6.1   Background Dialog Box

3.   Next to the colored rectangular window at the bottom, click on the *down* arrow to view several solid color selections. Select *Fill Effects* to observe the *Gradient, Texture, Pattern,* and *Picture* background options.

4.   To create a gradient background using the school's colors select the **Gradient** tab.

5.   Under *Colors* click on the button next to the *Two colors* option.

6.   Select the first gradient color beneath *color one* and choose the second under *color two.* Look at the different shading styles before selecting one of the variants, then **OK**.

7.   Click on **Apply to All** on the *Background* dialog box.

8.   To exit the Slide Master, simply select another view such as **Slide** or **Normal View**. In addition, the Master toolbar often

appears on the screen when the Slide Master opens. If available, select the **Close** button on this floating toolbar to exit the Slide Master.

✔ **Troubleshooting Tip:** If a previous background has already been selected, the gradient background will be hidden underneath. Click on the top left corner of the Slide Master to select the background and press the **Delete** key. The gradient background will now appear.

✔ **Troubleshooting Tip:** If using a title slide for a presentation, the settings will need to be applied to it also. Select **View > Master > Title Master.**

Adding a School Logo (Importing a Picture)

Scanned images and digital pictures can be imported into PowerPoint and inserted onto slides. Be sure to note where the images are saved before inserting them into PowerPoint.

Need a picture or image to insert? You can obtain pictures on the Internet. *Right* click on the image (**MAC:** Click and hold on the image) and select the **Save Picture As** or the **Download image to disk** option. Navigate to the location where you wish to save the file and click **Save.** Educators may employ fair use guidelines to use a limited number of images and sounds for educational purposes (see fairuse.standford.edu).

Select **Insert > Picture > From File** and locate the image. Press the **Insert** button.

1. Select **Insert > Picture > From File** to bring up the *Insert Picture* dialog box.

2. Use the top window to find the image on a hard drive or disk and click **OK/Open.**

☞ **Learn More:** To eliminate a solid color behind an image, select **View > Toolbars > Picture** and select the **Set Transparent Color** icon on the *Picture* toolbar. Click on the background of the image to make it transparent.

✔ **Troubleshooting Tip:** The Slide Master is not designed for adding titles and text. It is for designing a template only.

Saving a Customized Template for Future Use

Once a template is created with the Slide Master, it may be a good idea to save it for other presentations instead of re-creating it all over again.

1. Make a copy of the presentation by either:
   a. saving the presentation with a different name or by
   b. creating a new blank slide show. Select **Insert > Slides From Files** to bring up the *Browse* dialog box. Navigate to the slide show you wish to copy. In the *Slide Finder* dialog box, click on the slides to copy (their borders will darken) and press **Insert** (or **Insert All** to copy all slides in the presentation).

2. After making a copy of the presentation, delete all slides in Slide Sorter View.

3. Choose **File > Save**. The *Save As* dialog box will appear.

4. From the *Save as Type* (**MAC 98 & 01**: *Format*) drop-down box, select *Presentation Templates* (**MAC 98 & 01**: *Design Template*).

5. Double click the folder where you want to store the new template.

6. Enter a name for the template in the *File Name* box and **Save**.

7. To apply the template to a new presentation, select **Format > Apply Design Template** and navigate to the folder with the new template.

Creating a Class/Team Yearbook Slide Show

This could be used to celebrate the end of the year in a class or the end of a season for a team. First, identify one picture for every month of the school year or a picture for every team played. Use those as a background for a series of slides about that month or about that game. Next are two methods to add a picture to a slide.

1. Adding a Picture Background
   a. Select **Format > Background**.
   b. Next to the colored rectangular window at the bottom, click on the *down* arrow and select **Fill Effects.**

   c. In the *Fill Effects* dialog box, select the **Picture** tab and press **Select Picture.**

   d. Use the navigation window at the top of the *Insert Picture* dialog box to locate the images on the hard drive or floppy and click **Insert** or **OK.** The *Background* dialog box will appear. Select **Apply** to add the picture only to the current slide. The slide background is now a picture image.

2. Inserting a picture onto the slide. This option allows you to resize and manipulate the picture with the Picture toolbar.

   a. Select **Insert > From File.**

   b. In the *Insert Picture* dialog box, browse to find the picture and click **Insert** or **OK.**

   c. Resize the image as desired. If text will be added to this slide, it is a good idea to lower the contrast and increase the brightness of the picture. Do this from the *Picture* toolbar (**View > Toolbars > Picture**). Select the picture and then continue to click on the **Contrast** and **Brightness** icons until the image is lightly colored on the background. This will allow text to be more easily read.

3. Add comments and titles with text boxes and callouts. To add a callout, click on **AutoShapes** or on the *Drawing* toolbar and choose a *Callout* from the menu.

Creating a Looping Slide Show

On Back to School Night, a looping, self-running slide show is ideal to set up in areas where parents are waiting to conference or as an exhibit for others to view.

1. Select **Slide Show > Rehearse Timings**. The slide show will open on the first slide of the show in slide show mode with a timer. Press **Enter/Return** to advance through the slide show at the pace desired. When finished, a dialog box will present the total time for the show. Select **Yes** to save these timings. You can review the slide timings for each slide in **Slide Sorter View.**

2. Select **Slide Show > Set Up Show** and choose *Loop Continuously until 'Esc.'* Under *Advance Slides* make sure *Use Timings, if present* is selected.

3. View the slide show. It will now continue to loop with the timings until the **Esc** (escape) key is selected on the top left of the keyboard.

 Learn More: To present the show without the timings, select **Slide Show > Set Up Show** and under the *Advance slides* area, select the *Manually* button.

Adding Student Narrations to Showcase Student Work

Student projects such as stories, poems, and art are ideal for showcasing in PowerPoint. Students can add narrations to explain the projects. Stories and poems can be read by the student authors for a special touch.

To record a narration you must have a sound card and a microphone.

✔ **Troubleshooting Tip:** If there are other sound effects on the slide show, the voice narration will "mask" over them. If you are viewing a show with both added narration and sounds, only the narration will be heard.

1. Select **Slide Show > Record Narration**. The *Record Narration* dialog box will appear providing options for adjusting the recording quality.

2. Speak into the microphone as you advance through the slide show. A sound icon will appear in the bottom right corner of each slide indicating that the slide contains a narration.

3. A message will appear at the end of the slide show. Click **Yes** to save the timings with the narration or **No** if you wish to save only the narration.

4. To pause a narration, *right* click and select **Pause Narration** from the menu. Click **Resume Narration** to continue.

To delete a narration, select the sound icon and press **Delete**. To run a slide show without the voice narration, select **Slide Show > Set Up Show** and select *Show without narration*.

Application Ideas for the Classroom Teacher

There are numerous ways PowerPoint can be successfully integrated into the classroom and other educational settings. Here are some additional ideas:

▶ **Back to School Night:** Informative slide show conveying expectations, needed materials, curriculum, goals, and objectives for the year.

▶ **About the School:** Convey information about facilities, programs, equipment, staff, student achievement, and school needs.

▶ **Introductory Materials:** At the beginning of the school year or semester, cover classroom expectations, procedures, requirements, and rubrics for grading.

▶ **Daily Activities:** Eliminate much of the need for writing assignments and notes on the board each day by creating dynamic slides with graphics that can be used year after year. Some examples include quote of the day, math problem of the day, daily objectives, journal entries, and grammar exercises.

▶ **Daily Lessons:** Enhance learning by adding a visual dimension to daily lessons. Add a few graphics or pictures to supplement a story.

▶ **Discussion Questions and Review Material:** Develop an outline of important topics. Print slides for student review in an outline format.

▶ **Teacher Narrations:** Add teacher narrations to slides so young students can view slides individually.

▶ **Notetaking:** Teach notetaking skills by illustrating how to capture main ideas by condensing main ideas into a few simple words on a slide. Print slide handouts to aid students in notetaking, such as *Handouts (3 slides per page)*.

▶ **Quizzes:** Create everything from simple quiz questions on a slide to more interactive exams using, for example, the *Jeopardy, Who Wants to Be a Millionaire*, or *Family Feud* formats.

▶ **Learning Centers:** Students can advance through a slide show individually or in a small group that requires them to look up information, research, create a project, or answer questions.

Application Ideas for Students

Students can improve their speaking, writing, and communication skills by developing presentations in the classroom.

▶ **Portfolios:** Students can showcase their best work and add voice narration to explain and express themselves.

▶ **Research:** Develop research presentations of book reports and research projects.

▶ **Stories:** Give an autobiographical presentation to the class. Telling family, fictional, or historical stories with PowerPoint can also be effective.

▶ **Career Preparation:** Create career-related demonstrations complete with business plans within a mock job-interview setting.

Quick Review

▶ **Create a Customized Template:**

View > Master > Slide Master to modify all slides

View > Master > Title Master to modify title slide

▶ **Add Special Backgrounds:**

Gradient: Format > Background > Fill Effects > Gradient tab.

Picture: Format > Background > Fill Effects >
Select Picture

▶ **Insert an Image:**

Insert > Picture > From File

▶ **Modify an Inserted Picture:**

View > Toolbars > Picture

Set Transparent Color icon makes solid background
transparent.

Contrast and *Brightness* icons lighten or brighten the picture.

▶ **Copy a Slide Show (2 Methods):**

Save presentation with a different name.

Insert > Slides From Files

▶ **Create a Looping Slide Show:**

Slide Show > Rehearse Timings

Slide Show > Set Up Show >
Loop Continuously until 'Esc.'

Under *Advance Slide* select *Use Timings, if present.*

Index